Stephanie

Praise for

What If It's Wonderful?

"This hope-filled anthem from my dearest friend Nicole had me in tears from the first page. I cannot recommend this book enough. As a trusted companion, she guides us in a life changing quest to reclaim our joy. If you're ready to release the fear that often accompanies your hope and find your God given courage to celebrate, *What If It's Wonderful?* is the transformative book your heart has been waiting for. Join me in savoring these powerful words as we ask ourselves the brave question, *What if it's wonderful?*"

—ELISABETH HASSELBECK, *NEW YORK TIMES*
BESTSELLING AUTHOR, EMMY AWARD-WINNING COHOST
OF *THE VIEW* AND COHOST OF *FOX AND FRIENDS*

We often forget that joy is an intensely vulnerable experience and that celebration asks us to be brave. With words that sound like friendship and feel like courage, Nicole reminds us that delight is essential to our personal, relational, and spiritual growth. As both a marriage and family therapist and a person who is intimately familiar with the ache and joy of being human, Nicole is the right person to lead this conversation. Struggling to embrace joy and find the courage to celebrate? Pick up this powerful book!"

—MIKE FOSTER, AUTHOR AND EXECUTIVE COUNSELOR

"As someone who tends to anticipate every single worst-case scenario, this book was a breath of fresh air to me. Nicole's words remind me that joy and sadness can not only coexist together, but I can learn from both."

—JAMIE IVEY, BESTSELLING AUTHOR AND HOST OF
THE HAPPY HOUR WITH JAMIE IVEY PODCAST

"Using her extensive background as a therapist, Nicole Zasowski flips the script on failure, stepping out of our comfort zones and taking risks, by giving us the audacious permission to answer this life changing question: *What if it's wonderful?* Read this only if you dare to fully embrace God's good gifts and discover the courage to celebrate your life. The truths and tools in this book will stay with you long after you read the last page."
—PAULA FARIS, FOUNDER: CARRY MEDIA™,
JOURNALIST, PODCASTER, AUTHOR, MOM, AND WIFE

"I'm not sure how often the phrase, 'What if . . . ?' pops into my head and then sends me spinning in the possibility of all the heartache that the 'What if . . . ?' could bring into my life. Nicole teaches us how to shift our perspective from worry to hope by pointing us back to the wonder of Scripture. Through Nicole's winsome storytelling, current research, and Biblical truth, you will come to know a celebratory God, and in turn, learn to celebrate along the way. And all of us could use more celebration in our lives!"
—JOEL MUDDAMALLE, DIRECTOR OF THEOLOGY
AND RESEARCH, PROVERBS 31 MINISTRIES

"*What If It's Wonderful?* could not have come into my life at a better time, not only to address my own restraint when it comes to joy, but also the collective pessimism that surrounds us. This is not a victory book for those who want to deny or bypass suffering. It's actually the opposite of that. *What If It's Wonderful?* is for those of us who've known pain and have been in a withholding pattern toward ourselves, toward God and toward the world. If you're tired of holding back and trying to mitigate or control your own expectations and pain, this book is for you."
—AMBER C. HAINES, AUTHOR OF *WILD IN THE HOLLOW: ON
CHASING DESIRE AND FINDING THE BROKEN WAY HOME*

"This book is a must-read for anyone who has ever struggled to look toward the future with hope. As a therapist who has lived these words, Nicole offers a rare combination of hard-fought wisdom and expertise. *What If It's Wonderful?* is both the friend and the guide we need to overcome the fears that often keep us from embracing God's good gifts. Pick this one up! It will leave you challenged, encouraged, and changed."

—LAUREN CHANDLER, AUTHOR, TEACHER,
WORSHIP LEADER, AND PASTOR'S WIFE

"What if I fail? What if I'm disappointed? What if I get hurt again? We all know what it's like to look to the future and ask ourselves these questions. Wise, vulnerable, and honest, this book is the guide we need to embrace the joy that perhaps we've lost along the way. I have no doubt you will grow from Nicole's wisdom and bold example."

—LAURA TREMAINE, AUTHOR OF *SHARE YOUR STUFF. I'LL GO FIRST*

"Cynicism is easier and pessimism safer than the potential humiliation of hope, which is why we frequently rely on these false refuges. To some degree, we have all been pulled into this cultural current, but thankfully, Nicole Zasowski is here to snatch us back. With brilliant insight and brave vulnerability, Nicole examines the heartache, fear, and self-protection that stands between us and freely enjoying the gifts of God. I never expected a book about celebration to slay my pride and grant me such blazing clarity about myself, but here it is!"

—SHARON HODDE MILLER, AUTHOR OF *FREE OF ME:
WHY LIFE IS BETTER WHEN IT'S NOT ABOUT YOU*

"With amazing wisdom and insight, Nicole invites us to a journey of learning to dream after heartache so that we, too, can find the joy Jesus promises—a delight that leads us closer to the heart of God. Whether you're in the middle of a disappointment or have walked through one in the past, this book will welcome you into the abundant life God created you for."

—ADAM WEBER, LEAD PASTOR OF EMBRACE
CHURCH AND AUTHOR OF *LOVE HAS A NAME*

"When I, in the midst of my own tormenting storm, most needed it, Nicole swoops in with the most God-breathed word to fill these dry bones and encourage them to not only walk but run again. This is a sound message that will send waves for generations to come."

—KENNESHA BUYCKS, CREATIVE, AUTHOR,
AND OWNER OF RESTORATION HOUSE

"Joy can be hard to come by in a time like this. Nicole Zasowski combines her hard-fought wisdom and expertise as a therapist to create a practical book that's a boatload of fun to read. *What If It's Wonderful?* is a field guide to cultivating contentment and joy no matter how difficult your circumstances may be. As Nicole brilliantly reminds us, when the world is on fire, celebration is both a salve and a salvation. This book could not be more timely!"

—JONATHAN MERRITT, CONTRIBUTING WRITER FOR *THE ATLANTIC*
AND AUTHOR OF *LEARNING TO SPEAK GOD FROM SCRATCH*

"As a professional worrier and holder of low expectations, my heart needed the gracious invitation: *What If It's Wonderful?* Through relatable story-telling, Nicole echoed my own hesitations to embrace delight and led me along the path to experience the joy God offers."

—HEATHER MACFADYEN, AUTHOR OF *DON'T MOM ALONE*

"*What If It's Wonderful?* deeply resonates with my desire as an artist to delight in the everyday and rubs up uncomfortably with the temptation to brace myself for the next disappointment and to skip over celebrating for worry that it might be too self-indulgent. Nicole's thoughtful story-telling, wise expertise, and faithfulness to God's Word reminds us that celebration is a daily practice, a worthwhile way of living and thinking, and a mark on the heart of a person who has put her whole trust in Jesus. What a treasure this book is."

—EMILY LEX, AUTHOR AND ILLUSTRATOR OF
FREELY AND LIGHTLY AND *TWIRL*

"In today's fragile climate of perpetual bad news, *What If It's Wonderful?* is a must read for the soul who finds themselves stuck in disappointment and the anxiety of 'What if?' Nicole offers readers a unique combination of exceptional storytelling, Biblical truth, and the insightful practicality of a therapist; this is a unicorn of a book. I know you will discover—as I have in reading this book—that joy is something we can choose and participate in, even in the midst of difficulties. And maybe most impor-tantly, that it is safe to celebrate. You'll learn to face pain, experience joy, and take action to celebrate. Nicole will show you how!"

—TRINA MCNEILLY, AUTHOR OF *UNCLUTTER YOUR SOUL*

"Celebration is as old as the Bible itself but we have lost the art and nuance of how to do it well. Along comes Nicole Zasowski with a timely appeal for living a celebratory life. Her writing is sparkling; her wisdom, thought-provoking; and her invitation, irresistible. Cheers to living a life where joy is stalked, bravely and beautifully, for the good of all."

—JENNIFER DUKES LEE, AUTHOR OF *GROWING SLOW*, *IT'S ALL UNDER CONTROL*, AND *THE HAPPINESS DARE*

"This timely book is a roadmap to help us understand that finding the courage to celebrate is "not only possible, it is essential." Nicole is a loving guide on a journey that each and every one of us so desperately needs. A brilliant writer, Nicole's words tenderly draw us in to participate in Christ's hope regardless of circumstance, confront toxic messages we've received about joy, and understand how to celebrate and live fully alive in Christ."

—ANDI ANDREW, SPEAKER, AUTHOR OF *FRIENDSHIP—IT'S COMPLICATED* AND HOST OF THE PODCAST *COFFEE WITH ANDI*

"Nicole lays out a compelling case for celebration unlike any I have ever seen before. She takes our hand, walks us right up to the mirror, and sits with us while we stare into the truth that our whole lives are passing us by while we wait on what could go wrong. But in the pause of these pages, a new question emerges: Will we have the courage to lean into *hope* again? This book is both an anthem and a way forward; a light pointing us back to the thrill of hope on the horizon . . ."

—MARY MARANTZ, BESTSELLING AUTHOR OF *DIRT* AND HOST OF *THE MARY MARANTZ SHOW*

"I want to live in a world where we all celebrate for no reason and invite strangers over for s'mores. Nicole reminds us that sometimes you have to *do* the celebrating in order to *feel* like celebrating and that joy is not bound by our circumstances. It's also probably wise to have a therapist on hand—another reason why we all need Nicole in our lives."

—ELIZABETH PASSARELLA, AUTHOR OF *GOOD APPLE: TALES OF A SOUTHERN EVANGELICAL IN NEW YORK*

WHAT IF
IT'S
WONDERFUL?

ALSO BY NICOLE ZASOWSKI

From Lost to Found

WHAT IF IT'S WONDERFUL?

AN INVITATION TO RELEASE YOUR FEARS, CHOOSE JOY, AND FIND THE COURAGE TO CELEBRATE

NICOLE ZASOWSKI

W PUBLISHING GROUP

AN IMPRINT OF THOMAS NELSON

ISBN 978-0-7852-2650-5 (audiobook)
ISBN 978-0-7852-2649-9 (eBook)
ISBN 978-0-7852-2648-2 (TP)

Library of Congress Cataloging-in-Publication Data

Library of Congress Control Number: 2021947355

Printed in the United States of America

22 23 24 25 26   LSC   10 9 8 7 6 5 4 3 2 1

For James, Charlie, Annie: You are reflections of God's extravagant love. I love celebrating you.

My life flows on in endless song,
above earth's lamentation.
I catch the sweet, though far-off hymn
that hails a new creation.
No storm can shake my inmost calm
while to that Rock I'm clinging.
Since Love is lord of heav'n and earth,
how can I keep from singing?

How Can I Keep from Singing?

Contents

PART III: FIND THE COURAGE TO CELEBRATE

Foreword

I THOUGHT ABOUT IT A lot during the pandemic:

What could have prepared us for this? Individually—mentally, emotionally, spiritually. What could have strengthened me for this kind of fear, frustration, and life disruption? It wasn't that I wanted to conquer and subdue this debilitating season, but I just felt so incredibly unprepared and unchained. Maybe more so than anyone around me.

I was starting to realize that all of the things that I had feared happening in 2020 didn't matter anymore because they'd been eclipsed by this GINORMOUS PROBLEM that was collectively plaguing every person around me.

And all the hours I'd spent my mental, emotional, and spiritual energy fearing other things? They'd honestly probably weakened my capacity to respond when the world goes awry faithfully. The days I wasted wringing my hands, hyper-planning each moment and trading being present for having a perfect strategy—that would ultimately not come to fruition—goodness. I had so much regret about the state of my soul at the beginning of the pandemic.

2 Timothy tells us to be prepared in and out of seasons and I just felt so caught off guard; so unfit for the fight ahead.

Why am I writing a foreword for a book about celebration with such downer thoughts? I promise, I'm going somewhere. Because I think this book has the power to not only encourage and exhort us, but also to change our spiritual and physical lives.

On those dark days, when I wondered what could have prepared me for this . . . one word kept cropping up: celebration.

I think seizing every moment to take joy when it was available would have empowered me in a whole new way. I believe more dancing in grace, receiving affirmation, letting my hopes get up in the kingdom and its impact here on earth would have been to my benefit when all of the wheels fell off.

I wish I'd celebrated more. I wish I would have gotten in the habit of asking: *What if it's wonderful?*. I honestly wish I'd already read this book from my friend Nicole.

But now I know, and now I'm following her as she follows God to celebration. And there's no doubt in my mind I'll be better prepared for the inevitable pain, pressure, and disruptions that lie ahead in my life. I'm ready to seize the light, the beauty, the words of life, and the hope around me because pushing it away is not life-giving and it's not making me any stronger anyhow. In Jesus' name.

— Jess Connolly

Author of *You Are the Girl for the Job*

You're Invited

We praise you, O God,
for light in darkness,
for bonfires and beacons,
for hope and companionship
and bright waystations
on our journey.

"Liturgy for the Enjoyment of Bonfires In the Night,"
Douglas Kaine McKelvey, Every Moment Holy

THE SUN WINKS THROUGH THE clouds, creating a spotlight on our front yard. The sky bleaches from blue to white, warming to pink on the horizon, and the sullen sea lies flat in the distance after a churning August thunderstorm. I hear waves knocking against sailboats as they cut through the river to the sound. It's a faint hum but I am attuned to it. Flip-flops slap on the damp pavement—the blissful anthem of neighbors re-emerging to the day after the rain and making their way back to our neighborhood beach or to Brendan's, an ice cream shop that caters to the nostalgia of a time gone by. New Englanders insist upon savoring and celebrating summer, and I am becoming one of them.

My husband, Jimmy, is arranging wood in our firepit with precision, as if playing a game of Jenga, while I shove a variety of drinks into a bucket of ice: lemonade, several flavors of sparkling water, and some beer and wine for the adults. A large tray of s'mores supplies—dozens of graham crackers, king-size chocolate bars, marshmallows, and a large jar of peanut butter (I've learned this is an essential ingredient for some)—is displayed on our front porch.

Since the beginning of summer, we have held a Saturday night tradition of making s'mores at the firepit in our front yard. We provide refreshments, s'mores fixings, and lawn games. Sometimes I add large bowls of freshly picked berries that stain our fingers red and purple, sugar snap peas from our latest farmer's market haul, or buckets of fuzzy peaches.

No one is invited, and everyone is invited. What I mean is, there is no specific guest list or calls made, telling people to come over at a specific time. But neighbors, friends of neighbors who are visiting from out of town, or anyone who happens to be passing by on their walking route is invited to our weekly front yard party. Some quickly grab a drink before proceeding with their walk. Others find their way to one of the Adirondack chairs surrounding our firepit and share their stories, chatting and laughing with us and watching the fire's embers twirl toward the stars.

As we finish preparing our front yard, unsure of what this evening's celebration will look like exactly, one neighbor—an elderly man—passes by with his golden retriever. The man slows his pace and says, "Hi! What are you celebrating?"

We are well rehearsed with this question. Sometimes we say, "Summer!" or "Saturday!" But today—as we answer most often—we say, "You!"

The man smiles. His eyes, the color of the amber glass of a beer bottle, crinkle with obvious delight. He makes himself comfortable in an Adirondack chair, watching the smoke from the fire curl into the air and telling us his favorite tales about life in our neighborhood.

In the early days of this Saturday night tradition, the group that gathered was small—sometimes just Jimmy and me. It looked like we had prepared the festivities for a party that never materialized. But after several weeks, our front-yard firepit gathering turned into a celebration people have begun to anticipate. Some of our neighbors talk about the gathering and plan for it throughout their week. And I've even noticed a few walkers from other parts of town intentionally shift their routes to more consistently include our house on Saturday evening. Maybe they like the free sparkling water, but I think it's the fellowship and the festivity of the ordinary that they crave and have come to count on each Saturday. I have grown to depend on this excitement too.

"So why are you doing this every week?" the man asks.

"Because celebration is changing everything for me," I say.

These are words you would not have heard from me even a few years ago. Frankly, the idea of celebrating terrified me. Like so many others I had known—clients I had seen in my therapy practice, friends, family members—who had experienced prolonged seasons of hurt and disappointment, I had become highly suspicious of joy, afraid to hold God's good gifts for fear that they would be snatched away. I was sure that celebration always came with a catch, so I became practiced in praying for the miracle while preparing to mourn.

But I was beginning to understand that this perspective was costly. I realized that much of the loss I had experienced in my life was not only the grief and disappointment itself, but also the joy I overlooked because I was too afraid to embrace it. I was missing out on delight in the present moment because I dreaded the pain I imagined the future would bring. I neglected connection in relationships because too often, I chose projects over people. And, I was missing the enduring joy of deepening my relationship with God, often distracted with expecting more thrill from earthly victories, opportunities, and gifts than they were meant to give.

I also wondered about the purpose of celebration in our lives. Christians, at least the ones I stood shoulder to shoulder with through most seasons of my life, tended to emphasize other disciplines—like prayer, fasting, and the study of God's Word—but were not particularly disciplined about celebration. Without knowing it, I began to liken celebration to dessert: enjoyable, yes, but indulgent and unnecessary to the Christian life.

As a follower of Jesus, I had no trouble envisioning and embracing freedom in practices and virtues such as love, humility, service, faith, and even perseverance . . . but celebration? I had no imagination for how to actively pursue joy with reckless abandon. What did celebrating freely look like for someone who has put her trust in Jesus?

How *does* joy transform our hearts?

Can celebration help to smooth out the rough edges of our humanity? Can it grow us? Can it stretch us? Can exuberant celebration whittle character within us? How does delight keep us tethered to the hope of Christ? And if we are brave enough to hold on to joy for even a little bit longer than we've dared before, will we find Christ holding on to us in our celebration too?

The answers may surprise you. And I think they will delight you.

I didn't think I could be that person—the celebrator. This is what I know: finding the courage to celebrate is not a journey but a quest. A journey describes a passage of progress from one stage to another. There is a sense of openness as we wait to discover the meaning in our adventures and passively absorb joy along the way. I have nothing against journeys and have experienced many significant ones myself. But this book is not one of them. This is a quest—an active pursuit in search of something valuable and worthy of our attention. Because few among us simply drift toward joy.

During our time together we will need to make deliberate choices and take active steps in our quest toward finding the courage to celebrate. This might look like actually celebrating a win, trusting that God is as present in your joy as He is in your pain. Possibly, this will mean practicing celebration when you feel you don't have a reason to do so—when your prayers are threadbare of hope. Maybe finding the courage to celebrate means highlighting points of progress—personal growth in an area of your life that you've identified needs intentional work. It may even mean celebrating an ending—the end of believing a lie that has wounded you for years or walking away from an opportunity or relationship that feels good but is no longer right. It means that we are tenaciously searching for God's glory in both our tears and our triumphs. Finding the courage to celebrate means understanding that our joy is merely an appetizer for the riches we have in Christ, and the story of our sorrow is never the last story that will be told.

As we consider our personal stories, explore God's Word, and understand what current research says about celebration, we will . . .

- learn why embracing joy is not only possible, it is essential;
- get honest about our hesitancies and understand their emotional roots, illuminating a path to less fear;
- confront toxic messages we have received about joy and rather consider celebration as an avenue of growth and intimacy with God;
- examine Scripture's invitation to approach life with an expectant heart and receptive posture as we embrace God's good gifts;
- and understand how to stay emotionally healthy and spiritually alive in seasons of joy and celebration.

Most of the stories in this book are not the well-rehearsed "greatest hits" that play well in speeches or toasts at a party. Some of the accounts are monumental events, but many of them are what most of us would consider ordinary life: conversations, moments of everyday delight, or being surprised by joy in unexpected places. All of the pieces of my life that I share have had a strong hand in shaping me personally, in helping me find the courage to rejoice. My hope for you in this quest is that as you read my story you will see your own. The details will be different, but as fellow humans designed in the image of a celebratory God, we share the same invitation.

I've also included a discussion guide because I hope you will read this book in community. Celebration is both inward transformation and outward expression and has implications for our individual lives as well as our relationships.

Finally, I am praying for you. As I wrestled with this message, wrote it down, and prepared to share it with you, I felt burdened by the many friends, clients, and readers who have shared their own complicated relationship with celebration. I pray that this message transforms your heart and shapes your life in the way it has mine. I pray that you will accept the invitation to release your fears, choose joy, and find your God-given courage to celebrate.

PART I

RELEASE YOUR FEARS

CHAPTER 1

What If It's Wonderful?

No one ever told me that grief felt so like fear.

C. S. Lewis

"WHAT IF HOPE ONLY LEADS me to disappointment again?" I asked, wearily.

The afternoon sun slid down the wall of the western sky, casting long, finger-like shadows across my friend Blair's kitchen and pinking the light, making everything look sacred. I swiveled back and forth on a kitchen counter stool, my hair four days without shampoo, wearing cut-off shorts and a navy blue T-shirt with "Ben Rector is my old friend" printed on the front—a purchase from one of his concerts I had recently attended and a statement I very much wished were true.

Blair had invited me over for tea on a Tuesday afternoon. She is a cozy friend and has a smile that can be seen from two blocks away. There are no subjects that are off-limits in our conversations, and I never have to explain myself. She understands the first time, even when I don't use words. It's easy to remember I'm not alone when I'm with her. She is the friend we all long for in this life and the kind of friend we hope we are to others. Blair nodded, unafraid of my question. Though her nod was one of allegiance, not of agreement. She had fought hard for me with her prayers and loved me fiercely through my hope and heartache. She understood what the fine print on the box of pregnancy tests never tells you: the emotional side effects. Of course, the emotional impact varies for each of us. I'd taken hundreds of tests, absolutely sure that I was pregnant, only to see a no, or one lonely pink line, emerge on the test, leaving me feeling discouraged and disappointed. Then, there was the elation of the yes, or two positively pink lines, that we had celebrated a handful of times, only to spend subsequent weeks being monitored at the doctor's office and watching heartbeats slow to an eventual stop—our merriment ceasing.

Blair was one of the many faithful friends in Connecticut who had tenderly walked us through a season that was a bit of a potpourri of experiences and emotions for me and my husband, Jimmy.

In many ways, we were thriving. After five years of living in Connecticut, I now called this state "home" instead of merely considering it the place in which I happen to lay my head down each night. This was a process that resembled an adolescent dating relationship: fits and starts, passionate highs and dramatic lows, threats of calling it quits. But God was both patient and persistent in His pursuit of me in this place.

Jimmy and I had both grown professionally, working at jobs we enjoyed but consumed many of our hours. Jimmy commuted by train to New York City for his job at Disney, and I spent most of my waking hours in my role as a marriage and family therapist at a counseling agency in our town. I found this work to be fulfilling but still hoped to build a private practice of my own.

We had a strong community of friends—relationships that pushed through doors we are often taught to keep closed, helping us to explore our stories with honesty and compassion, and walking each other forward to new places of growth.

But thriving cannot only be measured by what you can see. Behind our smiles as we lived a life we loved, we were exhausted, grieved, and worried.

What was less obvious to many, but those close to us knew well, was the heartache of losing four babies to miscarriage. For the last several years, our days had been characterized by fertility doctor appointments, prayers of hope, prayers of lament, difficult decision-making, long phone calls to family, and tearful hugs with friends. Also, Jimmy and I grieved differently, which made us feel alone at times, though we were together, defending against the same heartache.

On one particularly painful day, after my doctor had called to deliver news that meant our baby would likely not make it, I sat on the floor of my office, my head leaning against the door and called my mentor Terry, a former graduate school professor and now dear friend in California. During our conversation he asked me a question that continues to be critical to my healing: "What has this cost you?" The question gave me permission to acknowledge and voice the additional losses connected to the main loss. The answers were dendritic, branching out in all directions, leaving no piece of our lives untouched. We felt disoriented in the death of dreams we carried for that child—visions that didn't simply vanish in the light of our new reality. It took more effort than usual for Jimmy and me to remember that we were on the same team and still characters in a love story, though it looked different than we imagined or hoped it would. Prayers became painful. We knew that God *could* but also wondered if He *would*. We struggled to know how to celebrate friends who were pregnant and care for ourselves too, knowing that statistically, their baby would probably make it and ours would likely not.

One of the most noticeable losses, at least to me, was the impact on my relationship with joy. The chronic loss had changed me and the way I interacted with the people and events in my life. Life felt unsafe—not physically per se but emotionally and even spiritually. I had become a person who was not easily delighted and entered quickly into a spirit of disaster. I didn't want this to be true about me, but I was terrified that hope would make a fool of me. I knew that God's power was not contained within the limits of my imagination, but I no longer felt brave enough to dream. I felt convinced that possibility was only an avenue that would lead to pain. And I was certain that celebration—if I were to receive good news—could not be trusted.

THERE ARE MANY FACES OF self-preservation when life feels unsafe—behaviors we use as a shield to protect ourselves from pain. You might blame someone else, thinking of all the ways the other person could be different so that you might feel okay. You could anesthetize your pain by binging on pleasures that numb but do not satisfy such as television, food, or online shopping, only to confront the same pain when the credits roll, the plate is scraped clear, or the bill comes. Or maybe you cope with your pain by becoming your own merciless critic, refusing to see, let alone name, anything good in yourself.

For me, when life begins to feel perilous, I mostly rely on control to keep the plates spinning. I imagine the worst possible outcome for an event and decide that this tragic scenario is actually my reality. In my profession we call this *catastrophizing*. I do this in hopes that no pain will surprise me. The problem here, of course, is that I not only anticipate the worst-case scenario, I live it in my mind. Some might even say that I choose it. This refusal of hope, joy, and celebration may not sound like control as we typically define it, but that's what it is—managing my emotions and becoming invulnerable to life and all its gorgeously vibrant emotion in the process. Other voices, like God's Word and the kind encouragement from people who love me, try to assuage my fears, inject hope into my heart, and allow me to borrow the courage I need to celebrate the joy in my life. I experience the truth as a balm for my fear-sick soul as I hear it in the moment. But the unfortunate fact is that the voice we hear the loudest and most often is the voice inside our own heads, which means that kind words from the outside remain just that: sweet sentiments that are easy for me to dismiss.

Still, there is a difference between feelings being real and feelings being true. I knew that the truest story I could tell myself, if I had the courage to tell it, was that God loves me where I am and is for my good, now and in the future, that He is with me and empowers me to do hard things. While I may feel confused about how to reconcile His promises with my pain, I know that God weeps with me and would love to celebrate with me. I believe that for the Christ follower, hope is always a good idea and will never disappoint. I believe that so deeply. I just so rarely live that way.

In Numbers 27:1–10, we are introduced to the five daughters of Zelophehad. Zelophehad had died, and it was customary, in this time, that the inheritance would be passed to his sons. But he had no sons—only his five daughters who were granted few rights and privileges in those days. The five daughters were terrified that they would be left with no inheritance and, therefore, no provision as their father had died and they had no brothers.

> *There is a difference between feelings being real and feelings being true.*

In a defining moment of courage, the women decided to approach the tabernacle entrance—a place of judgment by leaders and the place where the Judge of all the earth stood. They bravely appealed to the God they trusted to be a fierce defender to the defenseless, the fatherless, and the widow. The five daughters' hope was in God Himself, even above the law that they were taught to obey—a law that offered them little protection. Moses brought the women's appeal before the Lord and God granted them the justice they sought. Their courage not only granted them their father's inheritance but permanently changed the law for people whose circumstances might also leave them vulnerable. Zelophehad's five daughters chose faith in God over fear based on their own personal experience. What was my dread costing me? What was I missing out on as I acted on my fear instead of my faith?

ELBOWS RESTING HEAVILY ON THE countertops, I took a deep drink of my tea, and for the first time, my eyes took notice of a hand-painted wooden sign hanging above Blair's kitchen window.

"Has that sign always been there?" I asked incredulously. Clearly no one marched into the kitchen and nailed it to the wall while we had been talking, but I had been in Blair's house enough times to be surprised that I hadn't noticed it before.

She nodded slowly, curious about my curiosity.

The sign read, "What if it's actually going to be okay?"—a question that interrupted my worry and assumptions about the future I had voiced just minutes before. Tears trailed down my face, unbidden. I chewed the inside of my cheek as I thought hard about this question, as if the cute wooden sign actually expected an answer. This question felt like an affront to my fear and hopelessness, and I suddenly realized that my apprehension and self-protection had been quite wounding—as if someone had just flipped the lights on in a dark room and my eyes were adjusting to the scene before me.

The stories I had been telling myself—the stories that attempted to warn me that joy is dangerous and would leave me hurt—were draining the delight out of my days. The colors of my joy had become muted and the texture of my celebration, dull. These tales emptied the future of all wonder and filled it with worry instead. And they were causing doubt that put distance in my relationship with God and those closest to me.

This question was like a mirror held up close to my face and, in many ways, it was difficult to look at the person I had become. When someone shared their belief in me as a therapist and my ability to have a thriving career, my internal response was, *That would be nice . . .* Each time I became pregnant, friends would tell me they couldn't wait to hold this baby in their arms. I smiled and hopefully said something gracious, but inside I was thinking, *I hope you can . . .* Loved ones would share verses that offered comfort and hope as I struggled to dream. I wanted to believe those words were for me, but in an effort to protect myself I would think, *Those statements are true for them but probably not for me.*

I was ever ready with a sarcastic rebuttal for anyone who tried to celebrate with me. And admittedly, I was judgmental of those who enjoyed the experiences I wanted so desperately for myself. I often wore an attitude that said, "Must be nice!" considering the reasons I felt I was more deserving. I had become emotionally independent, unwilling to be vulnerable with how much I was hurting and how deep my desire was to turn to a new chapter in my story.

Reading the question *What if it's actually going to be okay?* grieved me as I began to consider that much of the pain I had experienced in the last decade of my life was not only the sting of the loss itself but also my refusal to embrace joy. Many of the missed opportunities, losses, and relational disconnection and tension came as a result of my inability to celebrate moments of progress, yeses, beauty in the present, and connection with people I loved. I don't want to look back on my life—my beautiful, wonder-filled, God-given life—and realize that I've mostly missed it while I was busy preparing for the worst.

I once came alongside a client who suffered from crippling anxiety. He was a young man in his early thirties who had experienced a great deal of professional success. Yet, despite the overwhelming evidence of his talent and competency, he approached each project and

I don't want to look back on my life—my beautiful, wonder-filled, God-given life—and realize that I've mostly missed it while I was busy preparing for the worst.

opportunity with absolute conviction that *this time* he would surely fail. He never enjoyed or celebrated any of the victories or accolades he experienced and lived in constant fear of his imagined impending failure. When I highlighted this pattern of pain and pondered what this cyclical habit was costing him, he simply said, "It's probably costing me a lot of peace and definitely a lot of joy. But Nicole, one of these days, I'm going to fail and I'll be ready for it."

WHAT HAS YOUR PAIN COST you? Perhaps as you grew up, the people who were supposed to stay kept leaving. As a result you feel chronically abandoned and you allow yourself to depend on no one and are always ready to reject someone before she can reject you. Maybe you've made the mistake you swore you would never make, either against yourself, or someone else. So, you walk around believing that you are less valuable or even worthless, that Jesus has covered others' transgressions but not the one as significant as yours, and you can't possibly allow yourself to be the recipient of good. And you certainly would never allow yourself to celebrate them. Maybe relationships keep breaking in your life—people have called it quits when commitment felt difficult—and you've never seen anyone fight for something good and right. In turn, you've never learned to stay in the ring and advocate for yourself or fight for connection in your relationships. It's easier to walk away than to face difficult conversations or to sit in your pain long enough to let it become your teacher. Or, possibly, you've never known a day without physical pain—at least not one you can remember. And because of this, you've assumed you were disqualified from living a full life. A life of purpose and meaning feels off-limits to you because of your own limitations.

Hope celebrates God's promises and delights in what is possible with Him.

Hope is not a denial of the cost. It honors the painful reality but does not fall to fear because it knows that what we can see is not all there is. Hope celebrates God's promises and delights in what is possible with Him.

I LOOKED AT BLAIR WITH a new realization. My question was an echo but it felt fresh and new to me. "What if it's actually going to be okay?" I asked aloud.

"Oh sweetie," she says with compassion, hope, and just enough gumption, "what if it's wonderful?"

CHAPTER 2

Broken Toys

Courage is the most important of all the virtues, because
without courage you can't practice any other virtue
consistently. You can practice any virtue erratically, but
nothing consistently without courage.

Maya Angelou

"HI, HONEY! WELCOME TO TEXAS!" The flight attendant's tone was as sweet
as her words as I deplaned my flight. She wore a bright smile with big
hair, which appeared to be styled with the goal of reaching just a little
closer to heaven. Despite my many trips south over the last few years,
the warmth and enthusiasm of the Southern people always took me by
pleasant surprise. I smiled and thanked her as I peeled off my down
coat. As I did, a pregnancy test flew out of my pocket and onto the
floor. I had forgotten I had it with me and was hoping the woman
didn't notice, but as I glanced in her direction, she smiled again and

said, "Good luck with that, sugar." I smiled, cheeks blushing with embarrassment, but accepted the goodwill.

Would it help if I styled my hair like hers? I wondered.

Most of my counseling work takes place in a small rectangular office above a pharmacy and a fish market in Connecticut. A few times a year, my work takes me south to the land of award-winning barbeque, sweet tea, and incomparable hospitality. This time to Texas. In addition to my weekly counseling clients, I work for an organization called the Hideaway Experience—a marriage intensive ministry in which my co-therapist and I work with a group of four to five couples over the course of four days. I once shared about the Hideaway with a friend of mine and after hearing about group marital therapy she announced, "That makes my armpits sweaty." It might sound intimidating, but I tell you with conviction that it is the most transforming, miracle-infused four days. I consistently return physically drained but emotionally and spiritually filled.

This particular trip was both a retreat and a training, a gathering to connect with other Hideaway staff members, to tell stories of breakthrough and God's faithfulness, and to hone our skills and think creatively about how we could better serve the couples who courageously show up to the intensives with frayed hope and pleading prayers. My mentors, Terry and Sharon, led most of the training portion and I loved learning from them.

Trainings for counselors are unique in that most of the time we don't sit and passively learn information or participate in exercises that allow us to discern our strengths and weaknesses or understand team dynamics. Instead, we often vulnerably share about ourselves—our family of origin, our deepest emotional pain, or the facets of our lives that remain raw and unresolved.

For one particular exercise, we were focused on metaphors. If harnessed correctly and used appropriately, metaphors can be a powerful tool in expanding insight, deepening truth, and enlarging possibility—similar to the way that Jesus used parables. The group had spent some time listening to one another's life experiences and we were now tasked with voicing any metaphor that came to mind as we reflected on the personal stories that had been shared in the group.

I listened from the outer circle as metaphors were assigned to others' stories. Some were humorous. Others added nuance to a seemingly simple exchange. And several served to name pain and expand possibility in the midst of difficult feelings and circumstances. I was mostly quiet, listening and learning, engrossed in story.

Deep in my observation, I was surprised when the man sitting in front of me—a colleague I hardly knew—turned to face me. The group was silent, attentive to this exchange.

"Nicole," he began as my eyes locked on his. "I realize I don't know you well, but I can't shake a metaphor I keep thinking about as I reflect on your story of loss." He hesitated again. "Particularly your loss around miscarriage and how unsafe it has felt for you to hope and to celebrate. Anyway, I wanted to get your permission before I shared."

This exercise was a vulnerable one, but I knew this group to be safe and I instinctively trusted this man's understanding gray eyes. I nodded my consent for him to continue, both eager and uneasy.

"I have this picture of you as a little girl. It's Christmas morning and you are presented with a beautifully wrapped gift. I can see the anticipation and excitement on your face as you imagine what might be inside. You eagerly untie the bow and open the box and the toy is broken. It is clear you feel grateful for the gift and love the toy but feel heartbroken that you can't enjoy it in the same way you hoped you would."

To me, the "broken toys" were not the babies or even the pregnancies. They were the unmet expectations, the disappointment, and the grief that characterized this season. The broken toys were my broken dreams. My eyes misted. I gave a subtle nod and whispered, "Yes, that's it exactly."

The exercise was working.

He wasn't done. "Then you are presented with another exquisitely wrapped present," he said. "You feel excited to delight in whatever is inside and you lift the lid of the box to discover another broken toy."

The mist of tears collected into pools on the rims of my eyes.

"It's confusing and it feels easier to not carry any expectation or excitement about what's inside the boxes," the man continued.

I nod, offering a faint smile—gratitude for his compassion for me and thankfulness for his courage to help me better understand what I thought was understood all along.

My mentor, who was leading this activity from the front of the room, continued what my colleague started. "What do you do with the broken toys, Nicole?" he asked.

I paused, considering his question carefully. Certainly, I wished the toys weren't broken. The contents of the box were different than I imagined and required emotional adjustment upon opening them. But at the same time, they felt too precious and significant to discard. I couldn't play with the presents in the traditional ways, and I grieved what could have been and was not, but they were still gifts to me. Though broken, they were priceless.

Yes, healing was required for the brokenness, but the brokenness was also healing me in important ways. I had found many treasures in the wake of missed expectations and hope deferred. I will never call the pain itself good. God is not the author of our suffering, and I don't believe He asks us to see it that way. Life doesn't have to be hard to be holy. But I've learned to let pain mold me into something new. The learning had required healing and time. But with these broken toys came precious lessons that can only be truly realized in the context of pain. I've learned to hold unmet expectations and keep my heart open to possibility. I'm practiced in searching for new growth springing from dreams that have been scorched by disappointment. I've trained my eyes to see joy woven through a story I would never have been brave enough to write for myself. And I have discovered that delight is indeed infused in that story too.

I have a different relationship with God than I did before. There's an intimacy between the two of us that's been forged from heartache. I no longer see His blessing as a reward that is given on the other side of a good performance. I see His gifts as a reflection of His goodness and grace, instead of a prize for my own goodness and grit. And this grace has changed me. I am more tethered to what matters. I now know the inimitable joy of connecting deeply with God and others instead of trying to get them to clap for me.

THE DISCIPLE PETER CAME TO know this joy through his pain too. On the night before Jesus' death, Jesus told His disciples—His friends—that they would fall away from Him. This statement felt far outside the realm of possibility in the light of the disciples' love for Jesus. Peter was sure he'd be the one, that even if everyone else scattered, he would never fall away from Jesus. But Jesus gently corrected him and told Peter that, in fact, Peter would deny Jesus not once but three times before the rooster crowed that very day. It happened just as Jesus said it would. Peter denied association with Jesus and each time he did so, scripture tells us he was standing next to a charcoal fire (John 18:18 ESV).

The detail of the charcoal fire is seemingly insignificant until we understand the end of the story. Again, the Bible doesn't tell us exactly why Peter returned to his work on a fishing boat. But we know our human tendency is to bend toward our old ways in our brokenness. Peter's pain led him back toward his past, where he was a fisherman.

Later, after Jesus' death and resurrection, He reappeared to a group of His disciples who were fishing on a boat. Standing on the shore, Jesus called out to them and asked them if they'd caught any fish. When the disciples replied no, He told them to throw their nets on the right side of the boat (John 21:6). When they did so, their nets were instantly full of fish. One of the disciples turned to Peter and exclaimed, "It is the Lord!" (v. 7 NIV). As soon as Peter heard this, he leaped into the water toward Jesus. Jesus invited Peter and the rest of the disciples to enjoy a breakfast with Him, cooking over a charcoal fire. During their conversation, Jesus asked Peter ". . . do you love me?" three times (vv. 15–17 NIV). And when Peter said yes, Jesus told him to feed His sheep. The relationship was restored.

The Bible does not call this a scene of celebration, but there are a few details that help us infer it as such. First, Peter's reckless abandonment in his pursuit of Jesus when he recognized Him is a clear outward expression of his internal joy and profound love for his friend and Savior. Second, the role of food in community and festivity is consistent in Scripture and this reunion was no exception. Finally, Scripture intentionally mentioned that this restoration of relationship took place by a charcoal fire (v. 9 ESV)—the common thread in Peter's three denials. Peter's place of brokenness became his place of restoration.

My pain is precious to me. My place of brokenness has become my place of restoration. The broken toys and the scars on my heart tell an important story about who God is and who I am as His daughter, just as the scars on Jesus' hands tell an essential story about our identity as God's cherished children. I've learned to sit easily in my suffering because it's where I've seen Jesus the clearest and felt His presence the closest. I've grown accustomed to looking for the face of God in seasons with constant vigilance, more prayer requests, and phone calls that deliver bad news. Would I recognize God in the light? Would I find Him standing close to me? I knew Jesus to be present in my sorrow. Would He stay for my celebration? My pain had drawn me close to God, and I had to wonder what would keep us together in the midst of my joy.

Releasing my vision for how my life was supposed to be allowed me to see God's provision more clearly. Pain had allowed me to recognize

Christ as my only enduring hope. I became more deeply acquainted with His character and learned to seek comfort in His presence. In the midst of stormy circumstances, I had found God to be my unmovable anchor. Would joy leave me unmoored? Would I know this hope without the heartache?

In this way, the broken toys have been an avenue of peace and joy in my life. Also, my brokenness had deepened my connection with others. My story has provided a welcome mat for others to share their own experiences too, offering safety that often takes years. Strangers talk to me like a friend, trusting that at least on some level, I understand.

I LOOKED UP FROM THE floor where I pictured that box of broken toys. After several seconds of pause, considering his question—"What do you do with the broken toys, Nicole?"—I looked at my mentor and said, "Though I am heartbroken, I learn to play with broken things."

I am good at playing with broken things. I like this about myself. I am grateful for my ability to survive and even thrive in the most unlikely of circumstances. Others have praised me for my strength and it feels difficult to imagine my tenacity without the struggle. Being the girl who can do hard things had shaped my identity in critical ways over the last several years. So much so that I earned the moniker *Seabiscuit* after the movie about a horse of the same name who was an underdog hero of sorts during the Great Depression. I felt proud of this nickname. I did not love the suffering, but I loved being considered strong and I enjoyed feeling brave. Though untrue, in some ways, it felt like my pain was the most interesting thing about me.

While I longed for my dreams to be fulfilled, I wondered about the usefulness of perfectly intact toys in my life. I worried that "perfect" is nice to look at, but it wouldn't move me, grow me, or challenge me to think. How could beautiful, unblemished toys have as much to teach me as the broken ones did?

I also worried about my ability to connect with other people. Would I remain a trusted friend in the midst of joy and celebration? We talk about the "struggle being real." Would my joy feel inauthentic? Did others find it easier to love me with my pile of broken toys?

Also, the broken toys felt easier to play with because they were known. Playing with something that was already broken felt safer than feeling afraid to love something that might break. No one enjoys grief, but I knew what to do with it. Joy felt like an unchartered channel of disappointment. Expecting heartache took away the element of surprise. I both longed for and feared receiving a different gift. What if I found the courage to hold a gift only to have it shatter in my hands?

> *Playing with something that was already broken felt safer than feeling afraid to love something that might break.*

Conversations with clients and friends over the years tell me that I am not alone in my fears surrounding celebration. Waiting for life to betray us and expecting disappointment is common among people who have experienced any level of trauma. When the trauma has yet to see resolve, many of us become hypervigilant to signs of trouble—even *potential* trouble. Here, it is impossible to celebrate because we are always focused on the looming doom. This hypervigilance is often successful in convincing us that preparing for the worst-case scenario is the most prudent choice. Your particular brand of struggle may or may not overlap with mine. Not one of us is immune to hardship in this life. You know what it's like to take a blow that makes it a little more difficult to rise to delight in your days and look to the future with an expectant gaze. Maybe you felt your performance was never good enough growing up, and you live with the expectation that others will always be disappointed in you. Perhaps your family has experienced unimaginable tragedy and the future feels treacherous. When you receive good news, you assume disaster is lurking around the corner waiting to pull gladness from your grasp. Or possibly, as a child, you were given the message that you were insignificant. When opportunities arise, you expect to be overlooked. You may even hide, assuming you wouldn't be chosen anyway. Our stories are unique, but many of us have experienced the same pain that makes us more hesitant to trust joy. Most of us can recall a moment, person, or circumstance that complicated our relationship with celebration.

As I REFLECT ON THOSE words spoken to me in Texas, I recognize that not only was I accustomed to broken things but also the disappointment and heartache were the only places I expected to meet God. Through that exercise, I realized that I had mistakenly begun to see joy and celebration as experiences that can only be found on the far side of a long struggle, if at all.

Disappointment and heartache were the only places I expected to meet God.

I have not often prayed to a God who is eager to celebrate with me—not because this isn't true of Him but because I don't often include joyous celebration as part of His character. Now, I'm wondering if we've drained all the humor, delight, and fun out of our ideas about Christ and the Christ follower. I'm afraid we are missing the image of God with His arms around us at the beach bonfire, slapping his knee in laughter when we say something humorous. Do we see Him crying tears of joy when He watches the look on our faces as we open one of His gifts? Do we worship a God who is like this?

I once worked with a woman in her mid-twenties in my counseling practice who recalled a picture that hung in a prominent place in her father's office—a pencil sketch of a laughing Jesus. "I remember it because it is such a different picture than the images of Jesus I was often presented with in other places," she said. "That picture helped me understand Him differently. I wonder why we don't picture God like that more often."

When I think about the marks on the heart of someone who has put her trust in Jesus, a few characteristics come to mind readily: remaining hopeful in the midst of struggle, honoring others above ourselves, embracing and showing love to people that the world has decided are insignificant or inferior, being Christ-dependent and humble in triumph. But someone who celebrates? Seldom do I list this among qualities of Christ-like character. Rarely, if ever, have I regarded celebration as essential to the Christian life. But what if the discipline of delight is also important to my growth as a follower of Christ?

Yes, God's purpose for us is worked out in messes, storms, and struggles. But what if it is also worked out in our dreams, our celebrations, and our delighted joy?

THE REMAINDER OF THE TRAINING passed quickly and I soon found myself back at the airport. I had shared a ride with several of my colleagues who scheduled earlier flights than I did and had ample time to kill in front of the flickering neon sign of a TCBY frozen yogurt shop.

I had promised myself I wouldn't take the pregnancy test that sat heavy in my pocket until I was sure what the answer would be. After years of grief, I felt that stick was unlikely to be the bearer of good news.

Perhaps it would not be wise to take the test without Jimmy nearby. Weathering the disappointing end of another hopeful month alone seemed foolish. On the other hand, my expectations were low and it was something to do. After all, it was in my coat pocket. How much can a *no* hurt if you've learned to never expect a *yes*?

I took the test in a tiny stall of an airport bathroom with my knees pressed up against my suitcase. I waited in the same position, somewhat distracted by the chatter from the other side of the bathroom stall door from passengers reapplying makeup and talking about how airplanes always make their skin dry.

I looked down at the test balancing on my knees. Two positively pink lines. Did I dare celebrate?

CHAPTER 3

The Shadow of Shame

When people say, "I know God forgives me, but I can't forgive myself," they mean that they have failed an idol, whose approval is more important to them than God's.

Timothy Keller

THE EARLY MORNING HOURS—WHEN I see them—are my favorite hours of the day. Creation leans in, eager for growth and open to renewal. The light is soft and the blooms yawn open, reminding us that we can begin again. The world bends toward the light, inviting us to do the same. But this morning, I resist. I bend the other way, back toward the dark. Shame restrains me, telling me that I am not worthy of enjoying a fresh start after what happened the day before.

"I'd appreciate your prayers. This conversation with her feels hurtful." This text I sent to my friend would probably not have caused much of a conflict if I had not accidentally sent it to the wrong person—the friend whose house I was at—the very friend I was struggling with in that moment. It had been a challenging season in our friendship, and I felt unsure about how to navigate the minefield of misunderstandings. I knew a good heart existed behind actions and comments that felt hurtful. But it had been difficult to see lately. Sometimes our conversations felt safe and supportive, and I remembered all of the reasons I loved calling her *friend*. Other times, she was unpredictable in her treatment of me and our relationship was beginning to feel hurtful.

I am conflict avoidant and this weakness is frequently brought to my attention. In my personal experience, outside of the therapy room, confrontation typically leads to more pain: the relationship is damaged beyond repair or the other person decides it's not worth it to stay and I lose the friendship altogether. So I've learned to soldier through my own painful feelings to keep the relational peace. What I didn't realize for many years is that silence and calm doesn't always equate with peace. We are quick to point fingers at those who explode in anger in reaction to their emotional pain, failing to realize that withdrawal and avoidance can be just as relationally damaging. My mistake was being unwilling to confront the conflict with my friend whose relationship I found complicated in that moment, and instead being willing to discuss the issue with a friend who saw my point of view from the outside. Now my text was sitting on the wrong person's phone.

My friend was in her kitchen and when she made her way toward me in the living room, I was hoping she hadn't seen the text. She had. I thought perhaps she wouldn't understand what it meant, and therefore not realize what I had done. She did. She was very aware that I had included someone else in my feelings and not addressed it with her directly. She communicated all of this information without words but with a withering look.

My face flushed hot and my heartbeat began to pick up the pace. I couldn't find the words that would fix it. I wasn't sure those words existed. I loved her and didn't feel ready to let go of the friendship. I was hoping she felt the same way.

"I am so sorry," I said. "I should have told you my feelings have been hurt."

"I wish I would have known and that you would have felt more comfortable telling me than someone else," she said, her tone more wounded than angry.

I understood. As someone who struggles with perfectionism, I have a difficult time separating my identity from my mistake. The only way to feel fine is to fix it, but there was no going backward, only forward. And in the absence of being able to fix it, I began beating myself up.

"I'm the worst. You have every right to be upset," I said.

My friend looked confused. "You're not the worst. You made a mistake that hurt me."

Was there a difference? I thought. When you live with the idea that a perfect performance is the only way to remain significant and secure, your personal value plummets with each mistake.

We sat on her couch, my friend settled into the cushions with ease, and me on the edge, upright and uptight. I told my story as kindly and honestly as I could—the ways in which I felt wounded by the relationship and all the reasons I wanted to fight for the friendship all the same. She listened with sincere curiosity, furthering my regret that I had not offered her this chance earlier—and that I had confided in someone else.

Confession and apology feel scary when you have told yourself you are only as good as your last performance. But there was no other way through to the other side for this friendship. "I'm really sorry I didn't talk to you and felt so free to talk to someone else. Will you forgive me?" I asked.

"Of course! I'm so sorry our friendship became a source of pain for you," she offered as she hugged me, celebrating the fresh start—the second chance—between us.

I suppose this was a new beginning, but I didn't feel like

celebrating. She was able to move on so easily and accept the repair that had just occurred between us. Why couldn't I?

ONE OF THE REASONS WE are hesitant to celebrate, of course, is that we feel we are not worthy of celebration. Shame prevents us from celebrating grace. We are stalwart in our belief that celebration must only come in the form of a reward. If *you* accomplished the goal or if *you* participated in the effort, then—and only then—do you get to celebrate. We have allowed the voice of shame to become louder than the message of the cross—the message of freely given grace—because we are committed to earning the right to celebrate.

The voice of shame is reliable in communicating several destructive ideas. One merciless message is that there is no celebration outside of what we earn, that we are unworthy without a pleasing performance. Shame whispers that our value is ours to prove and that our sin and shortcomings are ours to fix. Shame also forgets that the good things we receive in this life are gifts. We often refer to shame as a feeling. But it is also an action. It is choosing to speak false words to our identity.

We are committed to earning the right to celebrate.

Shame also places a filter on input from the outside, readily accepting negative messages without question and rejecting affirmation. Our brains are little help to us here. Neuroscientist Rick Hanson says that our minds are Velcro for negative information and Teflon for positive information.[1] Professor Roy F. Baumeister confirmed that positive feelings are weaker and more fleeting than negative emotions, which tend to linger and be stronger.[2] For instance, painful messages that we are alone, inadequate, and worthless will loiter longer in our brains than the truth: that we are valuable, prized, and full of worth. Most of us are quick to absorb criticism and slow to trust a compliment. Even if we believe the kind words in the moment, our brains will often work hard to invent reasons the compliment is invalid. Negative feedback tends to have more staying power. If we received a mix of positive and negative feedback on a project or performance, most of us will ruminate on the negative feedback on the drive home—even if the criticism was far outweighed by praise.

Most of us are quick to absorb criticism and slow to trust a compliment.

Paul described this phenomenon as a war, using a military metaphor when he said, "take every thought captive" (2 Corinthians 10:5 NRSV).[3] Paul is referring to the mind—not just our thoughts but also our hearts and souls, our entire beings.[4] To embrace truth, we must fight for it.

Each one of us has a story that shapes the specific pain we feel when we have been emotionally hurt. The open wounds on my heart are insignificance, rejection, and loneliness. What names would you give your wounds? Abandoned? Unprotected? Failure? Some of us would like to skip this part and I understand that impulse. Sometimes it's difficult to see the point in becoming acquainted with our pain. But knowing that these painful messages are particularly sticky in our brains is just one more reason that we must put names to our feelings. Because as one of my colleagues says, "We cannot change what we will not name." In other words, if we do not specifically name our pain, we will not know which exact truth to claim in response. And this matters because truth is not sticky.

You and I have to be disciplined in our practice of claiming the truth and persistent in sticking it on the walls of our hearts. We make the truth stickier when we practice naming the truth before we need it—before we are triggered by hurt in a circumstance or relationship, we say the truth about our identity and security out loud. Also, if we are anticipating an event or conversation in which we might be tempted to speak unkind words to ourselves, we can visualize that interaction step-by-step, name the feeling we might feel, and practice addressing that feeling with the truth. Saying the truth out loud is important because it keeps our brains focused. Our brains love to think about many things at once. But we can only say one thing at a time, making us more likely to follow through on the truth. Also, our brains process the information differently when they hear it instead of merely thinking it.[5]

Shame can shape our prayers too if we let it. If you're like me, you might hesitate to pray about any suffering or heartache you might have caused, resigned to suffer the consequences without any sort of comfort or help from God. Shame says that you must pay the price that Christ already paid. Even in our relationship with God, shame only allows for the celebration of rewards, not gifts, including the gift of grace that allows us to simultaneously grieve the extent of our brokenness and celebrate the expanse of our belovedness.

In our shame, we are inconsolable, giving those around us an experience of being simultaneously pushed and pulled. We crave the affirmation and validation but can't receive it. Yet, we hope others will keep trying.

Shame is also cunning in its ability to convince us that celebration always looks like self-promotion or that fun is frivolous. Shame is manipulative in getting us to believe that the *best* celebrations are always the fruit of our own effort. But really, shame is just pride in disguise—a misguided commitment to being our own savior.

Shame will never be an agent of restoration in relationships. It is tenacious in finding fault within and holds us to a different standard than other people in our lives. If I allowed shame to have its way, the cruel inner critic would have forced me to replay the conversation over and over again and threatened my connection with my friend. It may have even cost me the relationship.

Contrary to what shame would have us believe, we don't need a perfect performance. Perfection will never be the hope that saves us or the delight that bids us to celebrate. We need Jesus.

Shame made its introduction to us early in the human story in Genesis 3. Scripture tells us life was different in the beginning. Our relationships—with ourselves, others, and with God—were different. There was vulnerability with no shame attached to it, and Adam and Eve enjoyed contentment in the garden of Eden that we could never conceive of now. Their relationship with God was also unique. They knew God as both their authority and their friend. They relied on God, resting in His presence and provision and feasting on His goodness. Adam and Eve relished in the beauty of the garden but were forbidden to eat the fruit from the Tree of Knowledge of Good and Evil because eating it would result in a kind of wisdom that leads to independence from God, pulling them outside of that intimate, covenant relationship.

Then, the enemy in the form of the serpent introduced himself, speaking to Adam and Eve in a voice that made them question what they knew to be true about God and His care for them. The serpent was subtle in his attack, asking questions that planted seeds of doubt in their hearts about God's goodness and His generous love for them.

Succumbing to their distrust that God was invested in their good and the temptation to be their own god, they ate the fruit and instantly felt naked and ashamed. In their shame, they covered themselves with fig leaves. They hid.

Consider this. Before Adam and Eve sinned, in what we refer to as *the fall*, the reflex was worship, adoration, and obedience to the Father. The reflex after the fall was self-protection, self-celebration, and disobedience.

Most of us don't cover ourselves with foliage when we experience shame, though we might hang our heads or struggle to make eye contact. But we do protect ourselves in other ways, don't we? My work has taught me that there are four types of "fig leaves" we use to hide from the pain we feel: blame, shame, control, and escape.[6] Of course there are specific behaviors within each of these categories. I tend to protect myself by being self-critical and performing for approval—hallmarks of shame and control. Your reflex might be to reach for different behaviors. Perhaps you hide behind your anger or shut down, becoming invulnerable to those who love you most. We all hide. It's just a matter of how. And all of these behaviors—our ways of hiding—will reinforce our pain.

Unlike Adam and Eve, you and I sit in the privileged seat of knowing that Jesus rescued us by identifying with us as sinners, absorbing our debt, and reconciling us back to God. Jesus was stripped so that we could be clothed in righteousness. So why are we still hiding?

My hesitancy to receive the gift of my friend's forgiveness was a mere reflection of my reluctance to receive Christ's sacrifice—the blood He spilled on my behalf to cover all of my sins—past, present, and future. If we lend our ear to shame and insist on earning our own way, being our own savior through our own perfection, we deny the transforming reality of Christ's sacrifice and the freedom that followed—the celebration of grace.

Jesus himself talked about this freedom He longed to offer in exchange for our shame. In Matthew 11:28–30, he shared these beloved words: "Come to me, all you who are weary and burdened, and I will give you rest. Take my yoke upon you and learn from me, for I am generous in spirit and humble in heart, and you will find rest for your souls. For my yoke is easy and my burden is light" (NIV).

Jesus' words beg the question: Why did His audience feel burdened? A yoke was a wooden frame joining two animals—usually oxen—and used for pulling heavy things. Craftsmen in those days would often continue to fit the yoke to the animals until it was a *perfect* fit. If the yoke didn't fit properly, every step would be a struggle and the animals would tire quickly. However, a yoke was also a metaphor used under Judaism for the Law, as in the Pentateuch—the five books of the Hebrew scriptures that told the Israelites how to live under God's rule. Like a physical yoke, perfection was the goal—the way to feel loved and safe. In these familiar words, Jesus was comparing the freedom He offered to the religious legalism put upon the people by religious leaders of the time.

Shame is an ill-fitting yoke. It's not meant to fit. Perfection in the eyes of the law was never going to be the hope that saves us. The law was designed to build anticipation for the One who would fulfill every letter of the law. Our shortcomings are ours to confess. They are not ours to fix. Instead, we have been given the gift of a Savior who has fixed himself to a cross—cancelling our debt and reconciling our relationship with the Father. We cannot do for ourselves what Christ has already done.

So, if there is a barrier between you and celebrating God's grace, that is you, not God. Jesus granted all the permission we ever needed to celebrate.

MAYBE YOU ARE PRONE TO shame too. Perhaps you have relied on it to help you survive your most painful life experiences. You make yourself small before others can do that for you. Or possibly, you've observed this behavior in people who taught you how to be small. If you struggle with shame like I do, celebrating grace will feel a little bit like stepping into the sunlight at high noon after being in a dark room. You might feel warmth and recognize that you are exactly where you are supposed to be. And you might squint and struggle to see the pain in front of you at times. If we want to exchange our shame for the courage to celebrate, we must confess, repent, and learn to walk in peace. This is not to say that our failings don't matter and shouldn't be mined for opportunities to learn and grow. It simply means that our failure does not have the final word.

The consequences to refusing confession are not just spiritual or even emotional as one might think. A lack of confession has physiological effects. Studies have shown that confession leads to an improvement in our immune system, reduced blood pressure and more restful sleep.

Confession brings our pain into the light. Repentance holds us responsible for what we do with that pain moving forward. God has delivered us from darkness, *and* He invites us to celebrate the restoration with Him in the light where we will understand our need for growth, not as a threat to our value but as a map toward restoration.

Shame was costing me the very thing I feared losing most: connection. Celebration is only possible when we recognize our need. Maybe this is why I found myself leaning inward toward the dark this morning. Celebration that relies on the self pushes us to bend inward. Minimization of the bad news of our sin prevents us from celebrating the good news of our salvation by grace. But a life that rejoices in Christ's victory in the midst of our failures is a life that leans toward the light.

This morning, my fingers curled around my warm coffee mug, for the first time I notice the flowers had turned their faces toward the sun. I decided to receive my friend's gift of forgiveness and to also forgive myself, celebrating the new beginning that grace had given both my friend and me. I too am learning to bend toward the light.

CHAPTER 4

Protective Pessimism

We are suspicious of grace. We are afraid of the very
lavishness of the gift.

Madeleine L'Engle

THE FLIMSY WHITE PAPER SHEET wasn't enough to hide the rattle of my
shaking knees. Not even the reassuring touch of Jimmy's hand could
still them. After several pregnancies that ended in miscarriage and a
few ultrasounds accompanying each, sitting in an exam chair was not
a neutral experience for me. As a mental health clinician, I am careful
not to use the word *trauma* casually, knowing that traumas occur in
varying degrees.

Dr. Francine Shapiro is the creator of the trauma treatment, eye
movement desensitization and reprocessing (EMDR). She introduced
the concept of differentiating between what many clinicians now
regularly refer to as "large-T trauma" and "small-t trauma."[1] Trauma
with a capital *T*, referred to as "large-T traumas," are considered

horrific events or circumstances that we often picture when we think of trauma: prisoner of war experiences, severe child abuse, surviving a natural disaster. But there is also "small-t trauma," which can be one-time events or chronic patterns. These small-t traumas can be less obvious in their destruction but damaging to the psyche nonetheless. For me, sitting in exam chairs and looking at ultrasound screens fell into this category.

I had done my best to keep my expectations low, but the longing I felt to meet this baby growing inside me could not be suppressed. I was eight weeks pregnant and the picture on the screen would tell me everything I needed to know about whether I could continue to hope to hold this baby in my arms or if grief would scoop this baby away to be carried only in my heart.

I knew what I was looking for. The ultrasound technician may have the formal training, but I was educated at the school of hard knocks. The picture on the screen had never matched the one I dreamed about.

Rosie—the ultrasound technician—knows me well and is familiar with my history. Because of her excellent bedside manner and the relationship that has grown between the two of us under the most unlikely of circumstances, I refuse to have an ultrasound without her—a fact she both loves and hates. My doctor has learned to warn her I am on her schedule two days in advance so she can emotionally prepare. She had always prayed for the chance to give me good news—she had told me as much that very morning. The vulnerability of looking at a screen could only be endured if she was the one to navigate the experience. A nurse practitioner in the office, named Shirley, who happened to be a dear friend, was also present upon my request.

On a bulletin board below the looming screen above, there were pictures of babies taped to the exam room cabinets—ultrasound pictures of babies throughout the stages of development, ending with a picture taken shortly after birth. I had two thoughts: God is amazing. But would He do that amazing thing for me?

My answer to that question was *probably not*—a response that grew from the seed of my own experience and desire to protect myself instead of trusting God's capabilities.

YOU MAY TALK TO GOD with prayers that are rooted in God's omnipotence instead of your own disappointments and limitations. Your prayers might sound more often than not like faith instead of fear— fear that your needs don't fit into God's priorities, fear that you've had a string of yeses and you're due for a no (as if God is always working to balance the blessings), fear that you'll be overlooked by God, or that He's seeking to teach you something with a no. I know that none of these theories are true, but sometimes I allow these lies to infect my prayers. Maybe you have consented to the same ideas.

I have a friend whose feelings and tendencies resemble mine. She and her husband adopted a precious baby girl. The adoption went as smoothly as one could hope for, but my friend was suspicious of the joy when she welcomed her daughter into their home. She too had a story that led her to believe that celebration only comes on the far side of heartache. She has continued to do the courageous work of turning to face the light of hope, but it was difficult for her to trust God's gift in the absence of any obvious hurdle or struggle. It felt too easy.

Without intention and the discipline required to pull our minds toward truth and hope, most of our brains naturally veer toward negativity—like a car that pulls slightly to the right if your alignment is off and you let go of the steering wheel. Jimmy's brain might be unique or, more likely, he is more practiced in training his mind on hope, always leaning toward the possibility of what could be, of what God can do. Left on neutral, my brain goes negative.

Pessimism is more than simply a neuroscience phenomenon for

me. It is a trusted guard against pain. I stare into the future and believe that the worst will surely happen. I rehearse disappointment in an attempt to prepare me for what I believe to be inevitable pain. Too often, I have let my brain convince me that it is helpful to practice the potential pain instead of training it toward hopeful imagination. When confronted with possibility or opportunity, my first thought following any momentary excitement is often, *It will be terrible.* And all I see is evidence that supports my theory that what I hope for will not turn out well.

Next to pessimism, I carry the similar but different shield of cynicism. Pessimism holds a lack of hope or confidence in the future while cynicism doubts people's motives—or in my case, God's. I know that God is good, but I imagined that the "good" in my life would always look like broccoli on a dinner plate: good *for* me, but never something I felt excited about. One of the most painful fears I carried was that I would always be disappointed by the story God had written for me. I knew that God does not cause our suffering and He doesn't plot yours either. But I was terrified that His plans for my life—the things He allowed and didn't allow—would always be something I grieved. So I became cynical, assuming that the goodness in my life would always feel like growing pains.

> *God does not cause our suffering and He doesn't plot yours either.*

If you're like me—prone to pessimism and cynicism—you've justified these tactics by calling yourself a realist. You've convinced yourself that you are a practical person and allowed yourself to believe that you are the responsible one. Hope that requires you to extend your imagination beyond your five senses would be foolish. Dreams must be tethered to reality—measurable, achievable, and actionable.

We've assumed that this is just our personality. We toss our hands in the air while saying something like, "Well, that's just the way I am," as if this strategy of coping with pain is a foregone conclusion.

We mistake this trait as a part of our identity instead of properly understanding it as an area of growth. But much of what we like to call personality is actually reactivity. Certainly the research is clear that we are the product of both nature and nurture. God has created us uniquely and has stored purposeful gifts inside each of us. But the actions and attitudes we take in reaction to our pain are learned. A refusal to trust God's character over our experience and rejecting hope are both merely reactions that are not serving our personal growth or our relationships.

Possibly you've picked up pessimism and cynicism to protect against a different kind of pain in a story that differs from mine. Perhaps you have experienced events or relationships that have taught you that men are never to be trusted and you hold your shields of pessimism and cynicism against imperfect but undeniably trustworthy men, severing connection. Maybe you've prayed unceasingly for physical healing. The diagnosis doesn't disappear and the symptoms stay and it feels safer to assume that God has forgotten about you or simply doesn't care. Or, like me, you've grieved several losses, and it feels more prudent to never imagine, let alone expect, a different outcome.

You and I wouldn't rely on these shields if joy wasn't so scary. Joy takes us by the hand and leads us into an experience of vulnerability that quite honestly, takes practice to tolerate. Few among us are brave enough to fully embrace this state of being. For most of us, joy is accompanied by the dread that it might be taken away. Dr. Brené Brown calls this *foreboding joy.* I once heard her talk about this idea in an interview in which she said, "When we lose our tolerance to be vulnerable, joy becomes foreboding."[2] She goes on to say that of all the feelings we face as human beings, "joy" is the most terrifying.

In the midst of our fear, do we dare celebrate what is possible with God? What if saying hello only means that we have to say goodbye? What if it's a false hope—a mere trick of the light that is only masking the dark reality we've suspected all along?

Leaning back, I squeezed Jimmy's hand as warm jelly was squirted all over my belly and Rosie searched for the faint flicker of burgeoning life. I glanced at Jimmy, his face expectant and beaming. My eyes darted on and off the screen, unable to look for too long. Silence thick with the tension of hope and impending grief. More waiting. By my calculations, we were three seconds past doom.

"We have a heartbeat!" Rosie cried.

The room erupted in tears of joy. Jimmy wept with his face buried in his hands, lifting his head only to smile at me and laugh with delight. Shirley hugged us both, proclaiming God's goodness. Rosie's giggle sounded like a tension release, grateful as she was to give us good news.

I laughed too. But my laughter was different. My laugh was soaked in pessimism and sprinkled with cynicism. I wanted to join the group's joy. Was I the only one who understood the reality of our situation? A heartbeat was an auspicious starting point, but it was just that: a starting point.

My laughter echoed the sound of Sarah's laugh from Genesis 18. I imagine Sarah also found joy to be a daunting experience after so many years of unanswered longings. After years of being barren, three men that we understand to be angels visited Abraham and Sarah's tent. Abraham quickly told Sarah to bake bread for their guests while he selected a choice, tender calf to be prepared for the men, along with some curds and milk. When the men asked about Sarah's whereabouts, Abraham explained that she was just inside the tent. One of the men said, "I will surely return to you about this time next year, and Sarah, your wife, will have a son" (v. 10 NIV). Sarah was listening at the entrance of the tent and heard every word.

The Bible does not tell us how Sarah felt in that moment. But I can imagine the pain that came with that promise. Can you see yourself standing at the entrance of the tent? Do you choose delight or doubt? Do you celebrate or do you try to protect yourself from further hurt by turning to pessimism and cynicism instead? Does it feel irresponsible or reckless to take a chance on hope, to take God at His word?

Sarah chose pessimism. She laughed to herself and said, "After I am worn out and my lord is old, will I now have this pleasure?" (v. 12 NIV).

The Lord confronted Sarah's question with Abraham and said, "Is anything too hard for the LORD?" (v. 14 NIV). This is the question I must now ask myself.

When God promised a child to Abraham and Sarah—a son they would later name Isaac, which means *laughter*—Abraham laughed with delightful disbelief. Sarah's laugh was bathed in caustic cynicism. I recognized myself in Sarah's laugh—a laugh that knows God can but doesn't trust that He will. A laugh that wants to hear the plan before she will trust the promise and needs a guarantee before she's willing to embrace God's goodness.

Like Sarah, despite my desire for a child, I protected myself emotionally by deciding that delightful surprises just don't happen to me, as if God plays favorites and I'm just not one of them. I knew better, but it was difficult to imagine blessings outside of what I could manufacture for myself.

My laughter ran counter to God's invitation to Abraham—and to us. God calls us to have an expectant heart, a receptive posture, and to embrace His good gifts. In Genesis 13, God instructed Abraham to physically walk the outer boundaries of His gift of descendants that are more numerous than the stars—to enjoy the fullness of His lavish love and embrace it (v. 17). Pessimism decreases our delight in God's gifts. Cynicism lessens our celebration. In asking Abraham to walk the outer boundaries of His gift, God invited Abraham to imagine a reality that is inconceivable in his flesh and to celebrate what is possible with God.

I have learned that the best way to cultivate change in our lives is both insight and experience. In other words, it's not enough to simply understand truth logically. We must experience doing something different in order to create lasting change in our brains. Even a simple move like changing our body position can help us to claim truth that previously felt foreign.

If you struggle with doubt, this might look like praying with a receiving posture, palms open and facing upward. If you often experience fear, this might mean planting both feet firmly on the floor as you remind yourself of the truth that you are not alone and are empowered to make choices. I once worked with a client for which the simple act of moving from a sitting position on my couch to kneeling on the floor was the change she needed to prompt her to speak more tenderly to herself.

Many of us will never have the opportunity to walk the outer boundary of a large property or attempt to count the stars in the sky. But are we brave enough to keep our arms open wide to absorb the wonder of what God can do? Will we have the courage to unfurl our fists and lay our hands open, palms up, to receive?

This idea was interesting but terrifying to me all at once. Receiving more meant the possibility of losing more. Here and now, was God asking me to walk the outer boundaries of my own gift?

I STARED STOICALLY AT THE screen. There was more to do.

"What are the baby's measurements?" I asked. I had seen heartbeats before. I had never seen a baby measure properly.

"Let's see!" she said with anticipation as I braced myself for the inevitable. Grainy swirls of black and gray returned to the screen. Jimmy looked eagerly at the monitor, hopeful and expectant once again. I could barely face the direction of that rectangular box that had brought me so much heartache. I felt sick. *This is where the joy leaves us,* I thought.

"Whoa! You've got a big little one here! Baby is measuring *ahead* of schedule!"

Hot tears stung my eyes. I wanted to believe the good news. But my experience said don't be stupid. This is the part in my story where it usually falls apart. Sometimes the baby measures slightly small and we start doing very creative math: Maybe the baby was conceived later than we thought. Maybe these measurements aren't really all that accurate. We come back two days later and the measurements fall further behind. Our hope fades but the baby's heart still beats so we refuse to give up. We keep our eyes firmly fixed on this life with faith in what we know to be true about God. But after one or two more rounds of this, we hear the words we have feared for weeks: "I'm sorry. There is no heartbeat." I knew no other story.

Maybe that was the problem. My vision was limited to my own story. While pessimism is one of my trusted protectors, it is not *trustworthy*—for any of us. Pessimism is a means of control as we attempt to take the element of surprise out of our grief. But anticipation does not guard against grief. When we protect ourselves from disappointment, we will also protect ourselves from being delighted. In gazing at our own experience, we are unable to cultivate our spiritual imagination. Our line of sight is narrowed to scientific facts and we are confined to the limits of our humanity. Was I really willing to claim that this is all there is?

The author of Ecclesiastes gives voice to my feelings in the first two chapters of this book. The author is struggling with the sense that everything in this life is meaningless. He wonders about the purpose of our work and complains that nothing ever changes and makes the claim that nothing we do will be remembered. Why hope for something different? He uses the phrases "under the sun" (1:9 NIV) and "under the heavens" (3:1 NIV) to let us know that only the limited area of our human experience is being considered. The author is clear about the failure of this approach. Looking solely at what is "under the sun" will make us feel depleted. Holding nothing but our own experience will lead us to become frustrated as we cannot solve our own troubles, nor can we find the hope we need with this limited perspective. Instead of expanding our view of God and His infinite possibilities and enlarging our capacity for hope, attempts to solve our own problems only expand our view of the problem.

If we trust pessimism and cynicism as our guides, they will only ever show us more perspectives on the problem—different angles of the same despair. They will never allow our eyes to wander off the problem long enough to catch sight of possibility. There is no imagination for the possibility of a miracle.

BLURRY ULTRASOUND PHOTOS WERE PRINTED on delicate, wiggly white paper and tucked in an envelope. Shirley handed them to me, pressing them into my hands, holding her own hands around mine as if to not only secure the pictures in my grasp but also in my heart. She knew joy was a hot potato of sorts for me and I'm certain this was her gentle encouragement to actually hold the joy and feel the warmth of it in my hands.

Future appointments were booked and I fought against the temptation to mark those days as endings to this story.

As we walked out of the office, Jimmy laughed once again in delighted disbelief. My eyes caught his, borrowing a little courage to do the same before looking down at my feet. Maybe these feet could find the courage to walk the outer boundary of the gift God had just given us.

CHAPTER 5

Comparison's Cost

A man will speedily sit down and sympathize with a friend's griefs; but if he sees him honored and esteemed, he is apt to regard him as a rival and does not so readily rejoice with him. This ought not to be; without effort we ought to be happy in our brother's happiness.

Charles Spurgeon

THERE WAS NO REASON MY friend's good news shouldn't have been good news to me. Objectively, it was good news. But when I glanced at my phone between trips from the car to the house, hauling grocery bags into the kitchen, my face fell to a frown—an emotional reaction and not the measured response I wanted to have. Her text included a sonogram picture resting on top of a signed book contract and read, "Now that's a good day!" The text was punctuated by a winky face emoji, which I found annoying and unnecessary. I understood her desire to celebrate with me. I'd known her since childhood and we often found ourselves on parallel journeys—college acceptances, weddings, graduate school decisions, job searches, fertility struggles—and had walked each of these seasons and milestones shoulder to shoulder. Also, our interests and tastes overlapped, which made her an easy point of comparison.

My friend faithfully showed her support and care for me across state lines and consistently shared encouraging words in both my sorrow and celebration. We had given our best effort in fighting comparison by committing to praying, processing, grieving, and cheering for the other. This text was an opportunity for me to do the latter. Why did I find the cheering to be the most difficult of these options?

My feelings were not helped by the fact that by my estimation, my friend always wound up slightly ahead of me. I spent a lot of time somewhere between looking up to her and trying to live up to her. I couldn't and wouldn't deny the obvious blessing in both of our lives. But I also couldn't ignore what seemed to me to be the reality that circumstances in her life just looked a little shinier. And on more than one occasion, she celebrated while I bumped into disappointment.

It also didn't help that she was android beautiful and always dressed for a first impression. We all have our armor. Hers just happened to be prettier than most. And to observe her talents feels like unnesting Russian dolls—they just keep appearing.

Her friendship has been a source of joy over the years. A gifted listener, she consistently and patiently walked me around a problem, helping me to see it from new angles and gain perspective. She also has a generous spirit and offered me an abundance of her time, expertise, and ideas, for which I felt grateful. But there were elements of our friendship that I found hurtful too—or at least, irritating. She is quick to share her victory and often slow to connect with me in her more painful vulnerabilities, and she considers her habit of being late a part of her natural charm. Admittedly, she's had a few honorable mentions in my own therapy sessions.

My friend's news *was* good news. I just wished it were my own.

COMPARISON IS SUCH A FAMILIAR assailant to our identity that we hardly notice its intrusive presence anymore. Its perceived threat has been diminished by its regular appearance in both our private and public interactions. We talk about comparison as a habit to avoid in the same way we discuss the fact that we should probably start drinking more water or getting more hours of sleep per night. Everyone knows this fact and no one disagrees, but few among us take any action steps toward change. I too am someone who has been passive toward the impact of comparison.

Perhaps the most common side effect of comparison is its damage to our joy. I certainly experienced this to be true in my life. Often, our sense of satisfaction or dissatisfaction grows in relation to the other. We decide if our lives are worthy of celebration by measuring ourselves against other people. These words from C.S. Lewis highlighted its perilous effects on our identity in a new way for me. In the chapter on pride in his seminal book *Mere Christianity*, Lewis writes, "Pride gets no pleasure out of having something, only out of having more of it than the next person."[1]

Comparison would like for us to believe that we only have permission to celebrate if we are better than whomever we decide to measure ourselves against. Few things will dull your delight or weaken your wonder faster than comparison.

It's destructive to our relationships too, a habit that is both tempting and ruthless. There are no tie-games. There is no room to appreciate the uniqueness of both or all individuals. No one gets a trophy for participation. Comparison demands a winner. And it

Comparison demands a winner. And it demands a loser. demands a loser. Thus, this unhelpful habit offers us a choice between tearing down our own personhood or our friend's identity—even if only in our own minds. When you make the choice to compare, someone will get hurt, whether the consequences are obvious to many or just to you. Yet, it's difficult to celebrate others when the joy is something we want for ourselves.

I AM CHALLENGED BY GOD'S conversation with Moses in Deuteronomy 3. Moses had been the Israelites' leader through years of hardships and victories in the wilderness. Because of his disobedience in striking a rock in order to get water for his community instead of speaking to the rock as God commanded, God had told Moses that he would not be permitted to enter the promised land (Numbers 20:1–12). Now, Moses was so close to the land that he could spot the Israelites' destination in the distance. He pleaded with God one more time to allow him to enter the land he had been leading God's chosen people toward for decades. But God refused and instead instructed Moses to take a good look at the land, noting that he would not be entering it. Not only did Moses not receive the answer he was hoping for, but God also told Moses that His answer was final and that this would be the end of their discussion on this matter (Deuteronomy 3:26–27).

The Bible doesn't tell us how Moses felt during this conversation. But the emphatic *no* from God and the overall tone of the exchange leads me to guess that Moses felt discouraged and disappointed. I'm no stranger to painful "nos" and I'm guessing you aren't either. In my experience, receiving a no is especially difficult to accept when it's final—when there are no opportunities to continue the conversation, make a case, or prove myself worthy of a second chance. But what I personally find most challenging is what God says next.

Not only did God give Moses a disappointing no and end the conversation, but He also instructed Moses to commission Joshua—to encourage and strengthen him for the dream that would not be possible for himself (v. 28). Moses wasn't asked to merely accept that Joshua would lead the Israelites into a land that he would never see for himself. He was told to celebrate Joshua, pouring courage and strength into Joshua as his replacement.

Again, we are not given information about how Moses felt in this moment. But like me, I'm guessing you can imagine what this charge must have felt like—to prepare someone else for the dream you've been working toward and to celebrate someone else's gift or opportunity that you would love to have for yourself.

If I'm honest, I've found ways to be "okay" with others' success and blessings I've coveted for myself. I'm not proud to tell you that I've played the game in which you rationalize someone else's achievements by comparing and contrasting their life against your own. Whether done intentionally or not, this nasty mental exercise usually results in belittling the other to feel more secure in our own position.

The voice of jealousy is not kind. The conversations I hear among other women tell me I'm not alone. We see a woman who is driven in her successful career and tell ourselves that she must not spend any quality time with her kids. We see a family with financial means who enjoys a comfortable lifestyle and console ourselves with the assumption that all the wrong things must matter to them. We look at our friend who is particularly slim, fit, and beautiful and think they must be vain and self-absorbed. We find a way to be okay with others' success by measuring ourselves against the other and cutting them down to size or judging the story that led them to their place of arrival—a kind of twisted equalizer.

But God doesn't tell us to merely find a way to accept others' success. Our charge is the same as it was for Moses: to celebrate others' positions by pouring courage and strength into them as they use their gifts and chase their dreams, even if the dream steps on the toes of our own.

Celebrating others and pouring courage into them is easy when we're not competing. It is a much more difficult task if the joy is a gift or an opportunity we would love to have for ourselves. Do we feel threatened when we see blessing being given to someone else that we believe is rightfully ours? Have we convinced ourselves that we are more deserving? Are we the first in line to call a friend to celebrate the fulfillment of her dream—even if it's a dream that we share? Does it thrill us to see others' success come easily and frequently? While I nod my head *yes* in response to these questions, too often I default to comparison and jealousy—particularly when the outcome fails to fit with my own ideas about fairness.

As with any emotional pain I experience, it helps me to return to Jesus' sacrifice on the cross. When I am tempted to point my finger in judgment of what I deem to be unfair, or when I claim to be an authority on who is deserving of blessing, I am helped by remembering that Jesus traded me my death penalty for an eternal celebration with Him. I am the recipient of a joy that is anything but fair.

I've learned to see comparison and jealousy as the growl that lets me know I'm hungry—hungry for the One who is jealous for my soul. The truth for both you and me is that we will be satiated by nothing else.

So when we see our dream being built on the land of someone else's life or when our best efforts result in the praise of another person or when our formulas that tell us who deserves what fail, may we remember this gift and find the courage to celebrate others wholeheartedly.

How will you follow God's command to pour courage and strength into your fellow brothers and sisters? How will you commit to this charge when you wish you could celebrate the dream for yourself?

One truth that is helpful to us here is that there is no scarcity in

God's economy. Celebrating joy in one person's life will never come at the expense of celebrating another. His grace doesn't get divided but multiplied.

Our tendency to compare and our inability to celebrate others will also be mitigated by trusting that God is a flawless author. He always writes the best version of the story. But they may be difficult to recognize as such if the story doesn't match our expectations. The intriguing redemption to Moses' story is that he is one of the figures who stands with Jesus on the Mount of Transfiguration (Matthew 17), which was in the promised land. Moses does set his feet on the promised land—just not in the way he ever envisioned.

There is no scarcity in God's economy.

It helps to remember that God is writing a gorgeous narrative for your life. He has fashioned every detail of you specifically for that story. But our delight will quickly shift to dissatisfaction if we compare the story we are living to the one that someone else enjoys.

I LOOKED ONCE AGAIN AT the picture my friend sent me. The reality still stung as I wished the picture was mine. But as I looked at the image, I suddenly wondered what would shift for me if I viewed this picture as a celebration of what God can do instead of as evidence of what he hasn't yet done for me.

How could I not celebrate in response to the joy God had written in my friend's story? It was comparison, not celebration, that was seeking to steal from me. It is comparison, not celebration, that is emotionally expensive.

I waited, letting the celebration settle into my soul—to take root and grow something new. I wanted my joy for her to be honest and true, but I was also aware that feelings follow action. My call to love and celebrate with my friend couldn't wait on my mood. The best way to cultivate joy in my own heart was to invest in celebrating her now—and to be the friend I would love to have in this moment.

Flowers are my love language, and I do my best to cultivate a garden of ample supply in my yard. I cut a few sprays of pink roses and tucked them among a handful of faded blue hydrangeas. I wrapped the bouquet with strands of pink and blue ribbon and tucked in a note in between the blooms that said, "When are we celebrating?"

CHAPTER 6

This Is It?

> For though [something] be good, it may be loved with an evil as well as with a good love: it is loved rightly when it is loved ordinately; evilly, when inordinately.
>
> *(orderly, regular)* *(excessively)*
>
> *Augustine*

I SAT IN A PLASTIC chair in the front right corner of the classroom, legs crossed, left foot flopping up and down in nervous rhythm. It had been five years since I sat in this chair as a graduate student in Fuller Theological Seminary's School of Psychology and Marriage and Family Therapy, hand shot in the air, ready with answers and eager to please. I had returned to Pasadena to attend and present at a therapy conference that was taking place on Fuller's campus.

I'd bitten my nails raw in anticipation of this presentation and as I waited for my turn, time passed underwater. My presentation was two-fold: a lecture and a live therapy demonstration on the topic of forgiveness. I carried my typical public-speaking jitters during the lecture, but I was prepared and felt confident presenting the material. It was the live demonstration that I had anxiously awaited for months. This is different than a role-play. There was no script to memorize. There was no script at all. A real person with a real struggle joined me at the front of the classroom and I was tasked with demonstrating the therapy techniques I had just discussed in the lecture in a forty-five-minute session in front of a live and virtual audience of my professional mentors and peers. I had very little knowledge about my "client" going into this portion of the presentation and there was no way to prepare in advance for what I might hear or how I might like to approach the time therapeutically.

It was exactly as terrifying as it sounds. I've always felt uncomfortable being on display while I'm in process. I like to show others my final product—a well-rehearsed, edited, practiced version that I am proud of. But as a therapist, we are always learning and growing in our craft—like anything, I suppose. But therapy feels messier somehow. Unpredictable. Not in a bad way or a wrong way, but in a human way.

It wasn't that I didn't feel excited about the opportunity. On the contrary, being given the chance to present at a therapy conference for this community was a milestone I dreamed about as a student sitting in this chair five years ago. I felt nervous but also excited. In many ways, this was a dream realized. My mouth curled into a smile as I thought about the fact that the girl who sat in this classroom years ago would have been really proud of me.

My turn came and as I made my way to the front of the room, I kept reminding myself that I was not alone, that I had the comfort and inspiration of the Holy Spirit. I told myself that I'd still be Nicole and I'd still have my full value at the end of this session, no matter how it went. And I comforted myself with the reminder that at the very least, I could feel proud of myself for having courage—even if I felt far from brave. That's the other thing about being a therapist: like it or not, working with others is accompanied by a thousand invitations to work on yourself. And the best therapists—the wise ones—accept those invitations. That much I knew.

The presentation and live session didn't go perfectly. Of course they didn't; perfection is neither a healthy nor a realistic goal. I finished and instantly thought of many things I could have said and didn't, and several decisions I could have made differently. During a conversation with my mentor in preparation for the conference, I confessed my tendency toward this habit, and he replied, "There's no future in that." I tried to heed his wisdom now. It didn't go perfectly, but it went really well and I was courageous and gave it my best effort. And most importantly, my "client" told me I helped illuminate some steps forward.

I returned to my seat, breathing deeply and absorbing the moment and was a little surprised by two thoughts that came to mind simultaneously, separated only by punctuation: *This is it!* and *This is it?*

THERE ARE SOME MOMENTS IN life that seem to have a little bit of glitter on them—moments that prompt you to pinch yourself to make sure they are real and that you are the one living them. Unforgettable events, personally meaningful conversations, breakthrough, hearing good news, sudden and startling joys like surprise parties or gifts just because, the yes that changed everything, an opportunity to try something new—these are sparkly moments that often bring smiles to our faces, a thrill of excitement, and are remembered fondly through the years. These are instances that naturally prompt us to celebrate either internally with ourselves or in community. This was one of those moments for me. I felt joy in reflecting on this culmination of hard work and the fact that I had boldly tried something new and been willing to show up and bare myself and my work as someone who still has a lot to learn. I hope I will always be learning and growing as a person and as a therapist throughout my life and was proud of myself for being willing to share where I am now.

Maybe you are like me and you are inclined to race to chase the next dream, slay the next goal, and push toward improving for next time instead of pausing to marvel about how far you've come. Perhaps you've minimized the need to celebrate, your eyes focused on how much work there is left to do. Or, possibly you've told yourself that celebration doesn't matter because your joy is attached to some kind of earthly pleasure like an accomplishment or a milestone. Personally, I didn't want to do that anymore. I wanted to resign from the habit of treating my joys as disposable, dismissing them as unimportant, or discarding them in favor of pursuing a better version of the gift. I am grieved by the fact that I've stared down many of my joys and instead of embracing them, I've told them how they could be improved upon. No more.

And the other part of me thought, *This is it?* There was no judgment in these words. This question was not born from a lack of contentment or gratitude for the opportunity. It was merely my observation that the glitter on the shining moment I had just experienced was already beginning to flake off. My feelings about my experiences were categorically joyful and pleasant, just less potent in their satisfaction—less sparkly. I was keenly aware that this joy was meant to be a reflection, not a fulfillment.

Years ago, I worked with a client who was struggling with feelings about her significance as she pursued a job at a company with an extensive interview process. My client was ambitious and it was apparent from where I stood in her life that she was talented. But internally she wrestled with feelings that this job would somehow add to her value and finally be the achievement that validated her worth. After months of intense preparation and grueling interviews, my client was offered her dream job. When she announced this to me in session, I asked her about how her success fit in to our conversation about her feelings of personal significance. "You know?" she said. "It's kind of strange. I felt elated for about ten minutes—like this was the gift that would make me want for nothing else, and I still feel really excited and grateful, but not fulfilled." My sentiments exactly.

JESUS TOLD US THESE FEELINGS might accompany our victories and seasons of harvest. While Jesus valued celebration, He warned His followers *against* celebration when seventy-two of them returned with joy after they experienced success in driving out demons under the authority that Christ had given them (Luke 10:17–20). Can you picture the crowd of followers? They've participated in a miracle by the power of Christ, and I imagine them returning with a skip in their step, their heads held high, congratulating one another on their victory as they debriefed the events of the day.

But Jesus told them *not* to rejoice in this but to celebrate the fact that their "names are written in heaven" (v. 20 NIV). The followers' triumph paled against the gift of their salvation and the presence of God in their lives. Jesus was not telling them that the miracle was not good, or that their joy was wrong. He merely cautioned them to be aware that this kind of joy will not last. Their celebration was better invested elsewhere.

While celebration is a gift, it can be deceptive. The enemy would love for us to believe that the earthly celebration is not an appetizer, but the feast. Jesus is not dismissing or shaming His followers' delight. Out of His love for them, He's warning them that the ultimate joy is yet to come! As C. S. Lewis said, "We are far too easily pleased." How quick we are to settle for earthly joy, instead of being satiated by the joy that is yet to come.

Jesus had a similar conversation with the rich young ruler (Luke 18). The young man approached Jesus and asked Him what he must do to have eternal life (v. 18). He was wealthy and successful, and I imagine he found security in the formulas that had mostly worked for him in his life. At first, Jesus responded by reciting the commandments. The rich man was pleased to report that he had memorized and followed those laws from the time he was young. But Jesus called his bluff and tested the man's heart behind his obedience and told him that he must sell everything he has, give the money to the poor, and come and follow Him. But the young man was not able to part with his possessions for the sake of Jesus. And he went away sad.

Jesus didn't rebuke the young man's wealth. Instead, He illuminated the placement of God in his heart. He forced the rich young ruler to take inventory and determine the true source of loyalty and allegiance. The young man was unwilling to rearrange the treasures in his heart and decentralize his personal wealth and dreams. It's the spiritual displacement that caused him to be sad.

This type of inventory forces us into a spiritual reordering. If we are unable to do what is required, we find ourselves in a spiritual displacement. For years, I've read these passages and heard Jesus telling me to quiet my celebration in reaction to earthly joy—good news, personal victories, or professional success. In turn, I've assumed that these earthly pleasures weren't worthy of my attention or my joy. But Jesus does not shame our success or disparage our dreams. When God empowers us to victory or facilitates movement in our callings, it is not wrong to celebrate that experience. Life's pleasures are meant to be enjoyed! But we must know that their effects will not be enduring. Our accomplishments are meant to be celebrated! But we should be aware that they will not be sustaining. Celebrating the gift without worshipping the Giver will ultimately leave us hungry.

Earthly pleasures have value. But the inheritance we have in Jesus is an overabundance of riches. Through Christ, our inheritance is peace (Isaiah 9:7), renewed strength (Isaiah 40:31), hope outside of circumstances (Romans 5:3–5), and comfort (Isaiah 49:13). Our everyday delights, personal accomplishments, and dreams come true are simply a taste of the richness we experience in Christ. We should not expect more from our earthly pleasures than they were meant to offer. Delights in this life were meant to be our enjoyment, not our sustenance. In celebrating our wins, thrills, connections, and achievements, we can also celebrate that the resulting satisfaction is only a fraction of the joy that is available to us in Jesus Christ.

What if the dissatisfaction we often feel in our earthly joy is not so much about discontentment but displacement? It seems to me that what sits at the center of our affection will determine the satiation of our joy. I wonder if much of our discontentment is a result of our lack of willingness to decentralize our earthly joys and dreams. Passions, callings, and gifts will become idols if they are promoted in the wrong place.

What sits at the center of our affection will determine the satiation of our joy.

What treasures in your life need to be moved off-center? Is there a relationship with someone special in your life that has over time, become the source of your significance? Has your home changed from a place of belonging and welcome to a place of perfection and performance? Has your desire for organization turned into a need for control and become the foundation of your sense of security? Have you allowed your wealth or accomplishments to add value to your personhood? Is it your hard work or your heavenly Father that's made you feel safe? What joys in your life are standing awkwardly in the wrong position? What celebration in your life has eclipsed your celebration of God?

FROM WHERE I SAT IN that plastic chair, in the wake of the accomplishment I was celebrating, it was clear to me that the only sustaining elements of joy are those that matter in terms of eternity. Chief among them: the ways in which we become like Jesus. No gift is more worthy of our celebration than the person of Jesus and the presence of the Holy Spirit in our lives. No purpose will bring more joy than growing more into His likeness. The glitter never gets rubbed off of this joy—the joy that belongs at the center of our celebration.

Maybe Jesus warns us against the celebration of joys like success, momentary victory, and earthly gain because it makes it difficult to recognize celebration that will last. Jesus doesn't dismiss our dreams as unimportant or necessarily wrong. But in our unwillingness to decentralize our dreams, I'm afraid we have failed to recognize that Jesus is the fulfillment of everything our hearts long for: intimacy, belonging, joy, and worthiness. He is the answer our hearts crave.

In the five years that passed since I sat in this seat as a student, I gained perspective that helped me see that in living a life where all my dreams come true, I felt comfortable without Christ. It wasn't until we moved and entered a season that could largely be characterized by change and loss that life's joys began to reorganize and line up in their proper place. This no longer looked like comfort; it was better. It felt like peace.

CHAPTER 7

Where Is Jesus?

Where can I go from your Spirit?
Where can I flee from your presence?
If I go up to the heavens, you are there;
if I make my bed in the depths, you are there.
If I rise on the wings of the dawn,
If I settle on the far side of the sea,
even there your hand will guide me,
your right hand will hold me fast.

Psalm 139:7-10

THE LATE FEBRUARY SKY SCOWLED and the wind that day turned the world sideways. Grace had carried our baby boy and me through forty weeks of healthy pregnancy. As my doctor said: boring in the best way. Hope had held us together.

I lay on the exam bed in my doctor's office, my right hand resting

61

on my taut belly, waiting. Waiting for the doctor to enter and read the monitor and waiting eagerly for our son to make his entrance, earth-side. The radio played in the background. Kenny Chesney wanted to know how forever feels, while I just wanted to know how the next day was going to turn out. Until now, my prayers and efforts had been spent hemming my baby in, safe and growing. Now, I just wanted him out—not because I was particularly uncomfortable physically. I wasn't. But emotionally, I just needed him to be okay. I wanted to meet my baby, and I was so close that I was sure it was all going to fall apart.

Yet, I sensed that my son was not only a gift but also an invi-tation. I'd learned to trust God in my pain—to accept Him as my answer in ambiguity, to let hope heal my heart with or without my circumstances changing, and to allow faith to keep me afloat in stormy waters. I wanted to believe, to trust God enough to put my full weight on joy. But doubt had a loud voice, and I'd spent years letting it shout at me.

The nurse at my doctor's office entered the room and told me and Jimmy that the baby was fine for now (I didn't like the "for now" part), but that his heartbeat was slowing as I contracted, and they needed to monitor the situation closely. I had been monitoring my own emo-tional situation closely and decided that I had had enough. If I was a glass of water, the nurse's somewhat innocuous news was the drop that sent the water spilling over the edge. Through wide, watery eyes, my voice became a desperately firm whisper: "I need him out." To this day, I have no idea if she had a reason or found a reason to send me from the office to the hospital, but I didn't question the gift.

When we arrived, I dressed in the flimsy gown and slippers and took laps around the hallways of the labor and delivery unit. Both Jimmy and my IV of fluids were my loyal companions. The nurses appeared to be entertained each time I passed, looking just so pleased to be there. They complimented and confessed their envy of my slip-pers, which are really more like fur shoes. "Thanks! They're on sale at

L.L. Bean!" I cried out over my shoulder as I sauntered by. Jimmy just smiled, also amused.

Prodding my progress with labor was a bit like pushing a small child on skis on a flat surface of snow. You intervene, hoping to create enough momentum for him to start moving on his own but he never does. He moves exactly as far as you push him. That was me in labor.

After several interventions, my water broke and labor progressed. Contractions seized my body, causing my muscles to quiver. My knees knocked together and I laid my sweaty head onto Jimmy's lap. My parents arrived and then my in-laws, all ready and excited to celebrate their first grandchild.

Soon, the doctors encouraged everyone to leave the room and it was time to push. Jimmy caught sight of our son, and I watched Jimmy's face transform into an expression I immediately recognized to be wonder and profound love. James was here—safe and loved. Relief blossomed in my bones and the shaking receded like a tide. There are moments in this life that words can't reach. This was one of them. A joy that is both contented and celebratory.

"I've been waiting for you!" was all I could say, over and over again through my tears. The nurse lifted our baby boy and placed him in my waiting arms, skin to skin, face to heart, breath to beating chest. I wanted to drink him in and memorize his tiny features when he was so brand new. Jimmy burst into prayer like most gospel choirs burst into song. He thanked God for entrusting us with the gift of raising James and prayed that James's identity would be shaped by God's love and that he would always know his safety in God's economy and that he would put his trust in Jesus. Still, all I could manage was: "I've been waiting for you."

THERE ARE MOMENTS IN LIFE that slice our stories into "before and after." One might assume that the sting of loss and longing that Jimmy and I had endured prior to James's birth was the "before" and the joy of his arrival was the "after." But if my story has taught me one thing it's this: our hope is not in the gift itself—even the best gifts—but in the Giver. James is a prize, lovable and treasured. He was not the beginning of my hope. But as I held James, delighted by the weight of him in my arms, I wondered if I was beginning to release my fear, finding the courage to slacken my grip on control and be brave enough to hold on to joy just a little longer than I had before.

Our hope is not in the gift itself—even the best gifts—but in the Giver.

James was a treasure I would not trade, but I was hesitant to lean into reality and embrace the joy that arrived along with him—not only because I was afraid it would be taken away, but also because it felt foreign. I didn't want to be suspicious of joy. As my friend Jeannie says, I wanted to trust God with the gift He had entrusted to me. But there was a part of me that was looking for the shadow side of this gift. He was here, but would I get to keep him? I wasn't used to joy being served plain. Receiving the gift of my son at face value felt too easy.

The heartache Jimmy and I had experienced together over the last several years is not the story I would have selected if given the choice. But it was the journey that kept me tethered to the hope of Christ— the season that introduced me to more of God's character than I knew before. The pain had forged a different relationship between me and God—a gift I found and treasured in the wake of what had been broken and lost.

I feared that embracing joy would mean letting go of all the learning and growing I had gathered in the pain. Also, I wasn't quite sure how to place God in my joy and celebration. I cherished the relationship I shared with God in the dark and struggled to picture what this would look like in the light. My fear revealed my assumption that as the season of heartache faded into a period of celebration, my dependency on God—and therefore my intimacy with Him—would fade too.

I am practiced in mining heartbreak and disappointment for growth and goodness. I've been proving that for years. I never called heartache good. I don't believe that everything happens for a reason. Heartache just happens. My loss had helped me understand that my formulas about who deserves what and how to keep myself safe and how to prove my worth were largely false. Though painful, each miscarriage had deepened my relationship with God and acquainted me with a new aspect of His character. The disappointments gave me eyes to see delight.

But now, I was beginning to understand that maybe celebration is also an avenue of God's grace. What if joy, in addition to pain, has something to teach us too? I knew Christ to be tenderly close in my longing. Now, basking in joy, I could see for myself that He did not move from that position.

In Luke 1, Elizabeth recognized God in both her struggle and her joy. Scripture says that both Elizabeth and her husband, Zechariah, walked faithfully with God, even as they carried shame and grief in being unable to conceive a child. When the angel Gabriel visited Zechariah, he was unable to release his doubt and embrace the good news and as a result, was silenced for a period of time by God (vv. 19–20). Zechariah had known God as his comforter, but was unable to trust Him as his celebrator. He wanted proof before deciding that joy was a good idea. In contrast, Elizabeth readily received God's gift of grace in becoming pregnant with a son after years of infertility. She was not entangled by doubt, nor did she allow the dread of what could happen to cause disbelief in God

When her cousin Mary, who was also visited by the angel Gabriel and told that she was pregnant with Jesus—the living God—sees

Elizabeth, the Bible says that the baby in Elizabeth's womb (who we later know as John the Baptist) leaped for joy (v. 41)! Both she and her unborn baby recognized the Son of God in their celebration. Elizabeth is humbled that "the mother of her Lord" (v. 43 NIV) should visit her and said to Mary, "Blessed is she who has believed that the Lord would fulfill his promises to her" (v. 45 NIV).

I want to be someone who has a heart like Elizabeth—someone who recognizes God in pain *and* joy and is, therefore, not afraid to celebrate knowing that God is present and engaged in both experiences. I would like to look into the unknown and choose to wonder about how God will move. I want to be someone who can appreciate beauty without dreading its dark side. I would like to say yes to a dream without weighing it down with ideas about everything that could go wrong. I want to build plans with possibilities instead of problems. I don't want to feel afraid to laugh or cheer out loud in the face of good news. I long to step into the light and trust that God will meet me there.

Though the Bible is filled with tales of brokenness and tragedy, the heartbeat of God's living Word is celebration. The Bible begins with rejoicing in the goodness of God's creation, which we see in the repeated phrase, "God saw that it was good" (Genesis 1:10 NIV), as He formed and filled the creation. When the fall occurred, this goodness was broken and the world was introduced to pain. The promise of Scripture is that there will be a re-creation. Revelation says that we will celebrate a reality in which Christ "will wipe every tear from their eyes, there will be no more death or mourning or crying or pain, for the old order of things has passed away" (Revelation 21:4 NIV).

Jesus' life is also bookended by celebration. He entered the world in the humble quiet of the night, but the angels could not be hushed, singing, "Glory to God in the highest" (Luke 2:14 NIV). The shepherds hastened to marvel at the babe lying in a manger, and the three wisemen brought lavish gifts. And while pain and anguish were real to Jesus on the cross, the pain was not the point but rather a means to an end: the celebration of our rescue and reunion with God. How could I claim that God is only present in my pain?

TWO QUESTIONS I SOMETIMES ASK my clients (whom I happen to know are people of faith) when they share a personal story or offer some sort of metaphor in our conversation are, *Where are you in the room?* and *Where is Jesus?* They offer both me and my clients insight into how they are feeling about themselves and how they feel about their position in their relationships with God and other people.

May I ask you the same? In your scenes of celebration, where are you in the room? Where is Jesus in the room? I personally had done enough exploring in the dark—in the doubt and despair—to know Him to be a compassionate comfort in my pain. In my hurt, I was held—enveloped in love from all sides. But in a room full of smiles and cheers, I felt distressed and sobered by the fact that Jesus' position in the room was less clear to me. I believed He was with me, but I struggled to place Him. When I tried, I pictured Him as more of a passive observer than a participant in the group's joy.

Where is Jesus in the room of your rejoicing? Is He invited and included in your festivity? Is He central to the celebration or is He a bit of a wallflower in your mind? Do you sense distance or closeness from Him in your joy? Is God present in your play? Or is He solely available to you in your pain? Do you seek His face in your delight? Or only in your disappointment and dread?

If you also find the light of joy a bit disorienting in your life, it's possible that, like me, you've knowingly or unknowingly perceived God to be a bit of a killjoy. The God I walked with for many years of my life was always eager to teach me something, pointing out where I had missed the mark and challenging me forward without comforting me where I was. Not all of this is completely wrong per se; it's just incomplete.

What my son was teaching me already is that not only is God present in our joy, the Bible insists that He *is* joy and a habitual celebrator. He rejoices over His creation (Psalm 104:31). He celebrates the sinner who repents and the lost who are found—a point Jesus made clear through the parables of the lost sheep, the lost coin, and the lost son in Luke 15. He isn't separate from our joy but is delighted by it.

CELEBRATING GOD'S GIFTS DOESN'T TAKE US *away* from God. It draws us *to* Him. Joy is among the fruits of the Spirit we cannot manifest by our own efforts. It is the fruit of those who belong to Christ and have the Spirit of God inside them (Galatians 5:22). It is our joy in the Lord that allows us to relish His gifts in our lives. Said differently, our earthly delight is rooted in the joy of the Lord.

James was a gift—so obviously unearned and separate from my own striving. I had encountered God in my season of grief. Now, I was beginning to detect the faint edges of the face of God in the midst of my thrill. I felt elated and saw that God's presence did not leave me. I sensed the courage to celebrate budding in my bones and I trusted that Jesus would stay connected to me and rejoice in this gift—His gift—along with me.

PART II

CHOOSE JOY

CHAPTER 8

Love Lavishly

A Christian should be an alleluia from head to foot.

Augustine

ON A SWELTERING DAY IN August, my youngest sister was married in Santa Ynez, California. The wedding venue was someone's personal home and the owner had a fascination with European gardens, which was clear in the grounds' design. The ceremony took place along a tree-lined path on the property. Fragrant white flowers enveloped the whole space. Even now, I can recall the potent scent of the white rose petals that lay like a velvet carpet on the aisle. During the processional, Jimmy and I each held one of James's hands, who was the ring bearer, and did *one, two, three, scoop!* in order to get him down the aisle with no objection. Each time James's two-year-old feet flew up in the air, white rose petals would spray up with him in celebratory fanfare.

As was the case with both of my sisters' weddings, the ceremony was everything one would hope it would be: arrestingly beautiful, deeply meaningful, and memorable. Laura Anne—a stunning bride—walked down the aisle on my dad's arm to a violinist playing "Ave Maria." My middle sister, Brianna, and I served the bride and groom communion—a sacred honor I will always cherish. I stood next to my sister, straightening her gown and holding her bouquet. (No one tells you how heavy those bouquets are!) I looked out into a sea of faces, many of whom had borne witness to my own transformative moments growing up.

I get emotional, even still, thinking about the joy of watching my sisters love and be loved by men who value and appreciate them as much as I do. My parents raised us to be best friends and I feel grateful that that's exactly what we have become. Bearing witness to their joy on their wedding days are two gifts I'll always carry with me.

During cocktail hour, I took cover under a strip of shade and tried to appear comfortable in my heels, with my youngest sister—the bride—after she and her husband signed the marriage license. My dad wandered toward us and had barely uttered the word *wow* before his face crinkled, eyes glistening with tears. This reaction was not unusual for my dad. We love this about him, but it was unclear exactly what his emotion was connected to in this moment. I assumed that most of the sentiment was attached to the event of him having just given his youngest daughter away in marriage, and I'm certain this was part of the overall emotion of the day, but what my dad said next surprised me.

"The flowers," he said, pausing as more emotion overtook him. Both my sister and I were curious about his feelings surrounding a detail like the flowers that some might consider arbitrary to the overall significance of the day. "They just provided such a picture for me of God's lavish love for us."

While weddings and events vary and different elements are more or less important to different people, beauty matters. Choosing joy by noticing beauty makes a difference. Beauty found in nature—in the spray of white rose petals, in the angle of jagged mountains that preach God's magnificence, and in the purpling sky at dusk. Beauty found in our stories—redemption of what we had written off as ruined, brave truth-telling and transformation woven through stories we wish were different. Beauty found in our relationships, vulnerable honesty (saying, "I'm sorry. Can we try again?"), and radical acceptance and embrace.

Beauty doesn't matter simply because of what it looks like. It matters because of where it leads us.

We might be tempted to dismiss a detail like flowers as frivolous and unimportant. Too often, I think, many of us diminish beauty's impact by considering it superficial rather than significant. But beauty doesn't matter simply because of what it looks like. It matters because of where it leads us.

IN THE GOSPEL OF LUKE, we meet a woman who had learned that Jesus was dining at a Pharisee's home (7:36–50). Uninvited and unwelcome, she boldly joined the gathering, and standing in the presence of Jesus, she recognizeed Him as her Savior and is so overcome with emotion because of what this means for her sin that she wept. Breaking an alabaster jar, she proceeded to wash Jesus' feet with perfume, rinsing them with her tears and drying them with her hair—a lavish act of love. The alabaster flask was expensive and imported from Egypt and the worth of the perfume inside was three-hundred denari, which would have been a year's wages for the average laborer at that time. In the days of the New Testament, a woman's hair represented her glory and honor, showing this woman's humility in the presence of Jesus.[1]

The Bible describes the woman as "sinful," likely a prostitute (v. 37). Not only is she not formally invited to this gathering, but also many would consider her as not qualified to attend even if she were.

The jar she broke and the perfume she spilled were costly and likely purchased with her immoral earnings.

I can see the guests—the Pharisees and the disciples—gazing upon this demonstrative love with expectation that Jesus will reject this obscenely sumptuous gesture, especially from a woman like her—as an abomination. They are waiting for the reprimand that will rebuke her audacity and her wasteful ways. But Jesus stayed and received the woman's grand celebration of Him.

The Pharisees watched this scene through the lens of the Law and their own perceived moral superiority—their love and celebration curving inward toward themselves instead of outward toward God. They used Jesus' receptivity as evidence against Him, questioning how He can be a prophet and allow this embarrassing demonstration of love to be carried out by a sinner.

The disciples were also indignant, judging the waste. In their opinion, the exorbitant amount of money squandered to honor Jesus in this way could have (and according to them, should have) been used instead to clothe and feed those in need. By their estimation, serving the poor would have been a more practical use of the money that was now spilled all over Jesus' feet.

The Pharisees and disciples called the woman's celebration a waste. But Jesus called it worthy.

Speaking straight to the guests' apparent offense, Jesus used this moment to teach the others that love is the fruit of a person who has received forgiveness with gratitude. The more one recognizes the gravity of their sin and the extent of their need for Christ, the more they will be able to receive the gift of forgiveness. And the more forgiveness they can absorb, the more effusive they will be with their own love.

The word for *love* Jesus uses here is the Greek word *agape,* which is a generous, sacrificial act of love for the sake of the other.[2] The Hebrew equivalent used in the Old Testament means a spontaneous feeling, which impels us to self-giving or to seize the object of our affection.[3]

If, like the Pharisees, our love leans inward toward ourselves, or if, like the disciples, our love is disordered, our love becomes dangerous, and we will seize dangerous things. Anything—even good things—that eclipse our celebration of Christ become dangerous things.

The sinful woman's lavish love was not dangerous but sacrificial and rightly ordered—a celebration of her King. The act of pouring perfume over Jesus—her Lord—was a tradition that harkened back to the Old Testament when the people would anoint their king this way in the midst of celebration. This kind of love is a natural response to God's extravagant grace. And we can only celebrate this extravagant grace to the extent we know we need it. She saw no waste in pouring her expensive gift on Jesus' feet. Of course, what you and I know is that she demonstrated her love and spilled perfume on the feet of the One who would ultimately spill His blood for her soul—the most extravagant gift of all.

I would like to believe that I would be like this woman in this story. I think many of us assume that our response to Jesus would emulate her lavish celebration. In actuality though I often stand closer to the Pharisees than I care to admit. It's uncomfortable to recognize that my need for rescue and grace is equal to the person I experience as hurtful, or whose views I struggle to understand. We are often comforted by our own decency and, therefore, fearful of our own depravity, causing us to minimize our astonishment of grace. But the Pharisees' actions are an admonition that diminishing the bad news of our sin only prevents us from celebrating the good news of our salvation.

Maybe this notion that we are undeserving of God's grace doesn't feel like good news to you—especially if, like me, you've struggled to attach your value to your own accomplishments or reputation. Perhaps it echoes a shaming message you've heard before from an authority figure in your childhood.

But while I too am attracted to the idea of earning love and becoming worthy of celebration with my own goodness, I have come to see my lack as the starting place of my hope. We are undeserving. But because of God's incalculable love for us, we get to receive and celebrate His grace anyway. This means we can be both undeserving and immeasurably loved at the same time, relieving us of the burden of proof and inviting us to cease our striving.

I see my own heart reflected in the disciples' indignation too and Jesus' correction might be more confusing to us here. Doesn't Jesus instruct us to care for the poor and to be wise stewards of our resources? Didn't He Himself stoop low to enter the world and live humbly without the traditional elaborate trappings of a king? Even if Jesus showed compassion toward the woman, why didn't He admonish against the lavishness of her gift? Why was her extravagance not considered excessive?

Jesus' response to the woman's act of love was not meant to minimize the importance of caring for the poor. It wasn't a message meant to diminish our calling as followers of Jesus to steward our time, talent, and resources to give to those in need. Wise stewardship and generosity toward the poor are noble and right aims, unless they are elevated and celebrated above Jesus. This virtue should never prevent us from falling on our knees in wonder and worshiping Jesus with extravagant love.

As we seek to care for one another through our service, let us be careful not to narrow our generosity to exclude lavish celebration and extravagant love. Here, even practicality and frugality can become idols if they eclipse our worship of Christ.

Jesus' teaching in the Gospel of Matthew 23:1–39 echoes this caution. He instructs us to go beyond the righteousness of the Pharisees whose virtue is self-dependent, controlling, and manipulative toward others. Jesus calls us to a morality that is the fruit of the transformation that can only be received through Christ's love.

We tend to think of practicality and frugality as the face of spiritual maturity. We carry assumptions about what the lifestyles of the faithful should look like. We are prone to praise celebrations that are simple or find nobility in minimizing the significance of a milestone or a dream. And if you're like me, perhaps you too have considered celebrations to be self-centered instead of an avenue for appreciating and thanking God for His faithfulness and provision.

But spiritual maturity is not just biblical knowledge or following God's commands as the Pharisees believed. Perhaps most important, it includes deeply delighting in God. This kind of love is how I want to celebrate—a braid made up of my extensive sin, God's forgiveness, and gratitude for the extravagant love I've been given.

We will miss the heart of Jesus' teaching if we reduce our ideas of lavish celebration to dollar amounts or an impressive display or performance. Sometimes lavish celebration looks like sparing no expense. And often celebrating lavishly, making someone feel special, or creating a meaningful space or event has nothing to do with money at all.

> *Spiritual maturity is not just biblical knowledge or following God's commands, perhaps most important, it includes deeply delighting in God.*

You might celebrate a friend lavishly by thoughtfully affirming her character verbally or in a hand-written note. Celebrating a relationship might mean taking more time with a loved one than the scheduled hour you have set aside—even if it means your to-do list remains undone. Extravagant love might look like purchasing or making a gift for someone you care for that makes it clear that you have been paying attention to what brings that person joy and makes her smile. Sometimes lavish love looks like learning to love what matters to your friend or family member—even if it is of no natural interest to you. Or it might look like using your experience, influence, or connection to further someone else's dream.

Maybe you've been presented with the opportunity to celebrate and have allowed your sense and practicality to overshadow your praise. Or perhaps you're in a season of loss or longing and feel that you haven't been given a reason to celebrate. What makes me feel hopeful is that no matter where we stand in our circumstances, we are not disqualified from delighting in a God who gave us Himself. This celebration will not eliminate the sting of whatever your pain looks like in this moment. But it will change the pain when we can say, "Look what God did!"

AS THE CANDLES BURNED DOWN, the rose petals now crushed and fragrant in the lingering heat of the evening, my sisters and I sat with friends from all places and stages of our lives, touching the rims of our champagne glasses, and telling the truest stories we know about love and friendship and the God who thought of it all.

These lavish acts of love toward God and other people are not confined to a church pew or events like weddings. Many of the most deeply spiritual and celebratory moments of my life happened away from the church pew. And I love church pews. They happen when James lays his head on my shoulder at the end of the day, his sweaty, limp body molding into mine. They occur when Jimmy kisses my forehead as I pass him in the hallway, just to tell me that he not only loves me, but he also still really likes me. They happen with the rise and fall of the waves on my parents' boat—the place of my favorite childhood memories. They exist in the kneading and chopping in preparation for a meal or in tucking crisp clean sheets onto beds that will welcome guests to your home. We are physical beings. God made a physical world with intention. Beauty might seem trivial or frivolous or even too opulent to be considered good. But our magnetism toward beauty is no accident. God packaged our personhood in a physical body with shape and form that takes up space and can grasp, taste, and bump into the glory of the physical world.

The demonstrative love of the woman in our story and the extravagant beauty displayed on that evening have helped me to understand we don't celebrate lavishly because it's what we deserve. We celebrate with extravagance because of what we don't deserve and have received by grace anyway. Celebration at its very best is a response to God's goodness, not a reward for our own.

Beauty connects us to God's abundance. What scene gives you pause? What feelings steal your breath? What words make you weep in wonder? What details bring you delight? Your answers are not unnecessary or unimportant. Because they will always lead you to celebrate the One who matters most.

> *Celebration at its very best is a response to God's goodness, not a reward for our own.*

CHAPTER 9

Receive Affirmation

Oh God help me believe the truth about myself no matter
how beautiful it is!

Macrina Wiederkehr

PULLING UP TO THE CURB outside our friends Lindsay and Peter's house,
I felt excited to be doing something beyond our regular Sunday
routine—anything to change the trajectory of a week that some people
might refer to as a "dumpster fire." After waiting months in hopes of a
yes to an exciting professional opportunity, I received a really painful
no instead. Of course I opened the email that contained this news
after arriving home from a medical procedure on my thirtieth birthday
earlier that week. Ordinarily, I love the regular rhythm of Sunday that
faithfully reminds us to release control and ushers us into a new week.
But this Sunday I was grateful to be doing something that felt "other"
to my normal routine.

Lindsay and Peter are friends that feel a little bit like pajamas: your hug at the end of the day and your cue to breathe and just be you. The four of us had planned to go to brunch to celebrate my thirtieth birthday. I was physically exhausted and emotionally depleted, but I felt eager to celebrate something—especially if it meant that someone else would be cooking my breakfast.

After a winding car ride past classic white churches and horse farms, we arrived at the Bedford Post Inn—a charming inn and restaurant and one of my favorite places in all of the greater New York City area. I was secretly hoping the Bedford Post Inn was the plan. Upon our arrival, the hostess led us to our table on the back patio covered in wisteria. I don't remember if I saw the larger group of some of my favorite faces or heard the *surprise!* first, but my face instantly crumpled like a sack lunchbag, so touched by the gathering and grateful for the way God had loved me faithfully through this community of friends—proof that you really can make old friends.

We enjoyed vegetable frittata, freshly baked scones, and fresh fruit to the soundtrack of the clinking of mimosa glasses and comfortable conversation. The kind of God who brought life to dry bones made sense to me in this moment. I felt like He was performing the same miracle for me.

To know we are not alone in this life will never be the truth that cancels our pain. But it is a truth that significantly changes our pain. When circumstances speak of despair, relationships remind us of a security that is safer than certainty and a comfort that is not afraid of the dark. Life to dry bones.

As a part of the celebration, Jimmy had planned a time of verbal affirmation of me. As a person who often has to fight to find her significance outside of accomplishments, words of affirmation are a gift that I both treasure and struggle to receive. To hear what my presence meant to the lives of people I deeply loved and to listen to my friends name the gifts they saw in me out loud was a narrative shifter—a reminder that I am worth celebrating not because of my performance but because of my personhood. I was mostly able to absorb the experience. Though I felt thoroughly loved through the conversation, it took effort to maintain eye contact, to receive without condition, objection, or question, and to accept the gift of kind words that were unearned.

Still, there was a part of me that was a little unsure of what to feel or how to be. Was it really acceptable to soak in this affirmation of myself? Was it self-indulgent to receive this kind of celebration of . . . *me*? Often, it's easier to believe a story about our weaknesses and failures. Affirmation about ourselves can cause us to avert our eyes in discomfort and disbelief.

Maybe you love your birthday. You love an excuse to eat cake. You find great joy in opening gifts and relish the opportunity to mark the moment by reflecting on your blessings from the year. You see your birthday as a chance to take inventory of your life—to get really honest about what is working and what needs to change. You might even relish being honored—not for what you do but for who you are.

Or perhaps the attention your birthday brings makes you uncomfortable. Possibly you feel threatened by the idea of getting another year older. Or maybe observing the day you were born feels frivolous and indulgent and you are repulsed by the thought of being at the center of anyone's attention. Maybe it's a struggle to believe that our mere createdness is something to be celebrated.

ACCEPTING ANY AFFIRMATION OF WHO we are is often lost in the chasm between pride and shame. For some of us, our sense of significance is defined by attributes and accomplishments that we have allowed ourselves to believe are self-achieved. Outside affirmation has built our identity. To celebrate who we are instead of what we have done feels weak or like we are settling somehow. It's difficult to tolerate celebration of ourselves in the present with unresolved dreams and unaccomplished goals. Pride tells us that celebration is a reflection of our accomplishments.

You might avoid and decline opportunities to be honored because you fear appearing self-absorbed and prideful and, therefore, default to shame. You assume that to acknowledge gifts in yourself or to observe growth would be boastful. So to avoid appearing narcissistic, you brush off compliments and minimize others' praise.

I have often rejected praise and refused to celebrate myself because the kindness feels foreign to the lies I've claimed, the stories I tell myself about who I am, and what makes me worthy of celebration. I suspect you're a storyteller too. Maybe you tell yourself stories about why people stay and why people leave or tales about the reasons you haven't been chosen or were left on the outside of the circles we love to draw in our minds and hearts. Maybe your favorite stories to tell are the ones about the person who is the better version of yourself— the more disciplined, more creative, prettier, kinder, all-around-better edition of who you are right now. And he or she has become your constant and unrealistic point of comparison.

It will be difficult to choose joy when these are the stories written in ink on your heart. There's no room to imagine or reflect on the gifts God stored inside you when you commit to those lies. The truth about your value will always feel like it's true for someone else but not for you. The celebration will always sit on the far side of a dream realized or a goal achieved, a mirage of satisfaction. You will decide that joy was possible until you made that mistake—that mistake that invited shame to move into your heart.

Of course these stories don't change the truth. Your feelings are undoubtedly real. But there is a profound difference between your real emotional experience and the truth. There are three sources of truth: God, ourselves, and others.[1] All three sources are significant. God is the author of all truth. The Bible is filled with affirmations of God's delight in you and full of promises about your safety in His economy.

But the reality is that God has given us a choice in whether or not we will take Him at His word. The same is true when He speaks through other people in your life. You have a community—family members, friends, mentors, co-workers, fellow church members—who have seen and named gifts in you. They've expressed appreciation for the difference your presence makes in their lives. They've complimented and called upon your talents. Perhaps you felt joy in this moment. But affirmation's lasting effects will depend on the story you choose to tell yourself.

Choosing joy will be particularly difficult in the face of painful feelings. We all have life experiences and relationships that have shaped our wounds. Maybe you've been on the receiving end of betrayal by someone who promised to be faithful, consistently unpredictable behavior of a caregiver, or you've endured a chronic health condition with no promise of relief. I know that, like me, you have very good reasons for feeling the way that you do—feelings that make joy feel foreign. But once again, I take comfort in the fact that there is a difference between feelings being real and feelings being true. Because of Jesus' death on the cross and His resurrection, we can experience emotional hurt and know that pain is not the end of the story. Perhaps, given the options of pride and shame, shame is the more attractive choice because in being self-deprecating, we feel less self-absorbed. But the truth is, shame is just as self-absorbed as pride. Whether you choose to inflate your ego or deflate your ego, pride and shame will both ensure that you remain focused on yourself. There is no nobility in claiming a worthless identity. Neither pride nor shame empowers us to choose joy. We need a different way.

There is no nobility in claiming a worthless identity.

Pride celebrates who we are apart from Christ. Shame refuses to celebrate what Christ has done on our behalf. But true humility celebrates who we are *in Christ*. Both pride and shame are focused on what we deserve and find safety in what can be earned. The freedom of humility is realizing what we don't deserve and can't earn but are given anyway.

It might require some nerve to stare into the extent of our brokenness. But many of us underestimate the courage that is required to gaze into the expanse of our belovedness. What if allowing our souls to feel their worth was a cornerstone of courage?

I once had the privilege of working with a young man who constantly wrestled with feelings of failure and worthlessness, largely resulting from his relationship with a dad who consistently told him how he and his work could be improved upon. Despite my client's laborious efforts, he never felt like he could measure up to his father's expectations. Despite having several meaningful relationships in which he felt loved and a long list of accomplishments early in his career, the young man was committed to the narrative that he wasn't good enough. He even admitted that he could never receive affirmation in his personal or professional life. When I asked what sense he made of this, the young man astutely said, "I guess I keep wishing my dad would call me up and tell me he was wrong—that he would correct the statements he made about me as a boy and just tell me that he's proud of me." From there, we began the difficult but worthy work of learning to parent himself the way his dad never could—to choose the joy of his worthiness.

Both the stories of creation and the cross extend an invitation to see our significance. When God created the beauty of the world we enjoy, shaping creation from formless and empty space and breathing life into creatures big and small, He chose to pronounce every piece of His creation "good." When God spoke, "it was so" (Genesis 1:7 NIV) and "God saw that it was good" (v. 10 NIV)—a phrase repeated throughout Genesis 1, he created the beauty we relish. The separation of light and darkness, sea and sky were good. Plants that grow, bloom, and bear fruit and sun, moon, and stars that hang as lights in the vault of the sky were good. On God's command, the water teemed with living creatures and animals roamed the land and God saw they were good. Finally, God made humans—His children—in the likeness of the triune God and blessed them, and He saw His creation was good.

The first chapter of Genesis is not merely a historical account of how the world was made. He celebrated us as His beloved. Often, as Christians, the early chapters of Genesis serve as an opportunity to confront the reality of our brokenness as we consider the fall when Adam and Eve disobeyed God and sin entered the world. And to be clear, our brokenness is both true and essential to understand if we wish to absorb the full hope of the gospel. But in the biblical narrative, our brokenness is best understood by first acknowledging our belovedness. Image bearers is the identity we celebrate as His beloved. This was our starting place. And the Voice that calls you and me *beloved* must be the primary voice we hear moving forward.

The cross is yet another invitation to choose the joy of being cherished by God. Romans 8:1 offers this promise: "Therefore, there is now no condemnation for those who are in Christ Jesus" (NIV). This is the Good News. God considered us "good" when He created us, and we are seen as good once again because by grace our sin is covered by the blood of His Son.

An honest look at your life will reveal weaknesses in your character, areas in which you need to grow, events and relationships gone awry. But there is no part of you or your story that disqualifies you from the promise that you are priceless.

This is our permission—our encouragement—to believe the beautiful truth about ourselves. We are free to confess our sin and free to speak honestly about our gifts and accomplishments, knowing that we are ultimately defined by God's delight and celebration of us as His children. Celebrating who we are means acknowledging the reality of our failures and the truth of our gifting and feeling joy about who we are apart from both.

Celebrating the person we are requires both time and intention. As my mentor, Terry, often says, "The brain goes where it knows." Getting your brain to agree to venture into the unchartered territory of celebration—particularly, choosing to find enjoyment in who you are—will not happen simply because you think it sounds like a good idea. This requires effort and discipline.

One place to start is by paying attention to your response toward affirmation. Do you qualify others' kindness by making statements like, "Oh, you're just being sweet." Or do you diminish the truth in someone's compliment toward you with a response along the lines of, "Well, I guess you're catching me on a good day." Or maybe you deflect the affirmation with sarcasm, saying something like, "You should ask my spouse and kids what they think!"

My work at the Hideaway Experience, a marriage intensive experience, has taught me a great deal about receiving affirmation. Toward the end of our four days of working together, there is a time of affirmation before everyone departs for home. Many years' worth of groups have helped us understand that receiving personal affirmation is challenging for most people, so we set up some guidelines, and one rule is particularly important: the only words you are allowed to give in response to affirmation are "Thank you. I receive that." While I don't always use these exact words every time, I have done my best to adopt this tenet in my own life. When someone offers me kind words, I make every effort not to judge the statement, question it, qualify it, deflect it, or reject it. I try to simply say some version of "Thank you. I receive that."

Taking it a step further, we are empowered to tell ourselves a different story—the truth about our identity. A warning: don't wait to feel this truth before you are willing to speak it and claim it as your own. Actions don't follow feelings. Feelings follow actions. Join the chorus in telling the story you know and not simply the one you feel. Often, we have to choose the joy we hope to feel.

Delighting in others will be helpful in seeing value in ourselves. Surprisingly, one of the marks on a person's life who has learned to celebrate themselves is their ability to celebrate other people. When we are neither drawing attention to ourselves by proving ourselves with our pride or by shaming ourselves in our insecurity, our gaze is free to focus outward.

Actions don't follow feelings. Feelings follow actions.

In *The Freedom of Self Forgetfulness,* Timothy Keller noted that C. S. Lewis recognized this to be true as well, saying, "The thing we would remember from meeting a truly gospel-humble person is how much they seemed to be totally interested in us. Because the essence of gospel-humility is not thinking more of myself or thinking less of myself, it is thinking of myself less."[2]

LOOKING AROUND THE TABLE AT the Bedford Post Inn, I reflected on each of these companions that God had encircled me with for this time. My favorite dessert, key lime pie, was served as puffy white clouds drifted across the periwinkle sky looking a little bit like they belonged in a Pixar movie—animated and perfect. These were the people I could call and say the thing I was not brave enough to say to anyone else, knowing that they will see my heart accurately and understand what I mean. These were the friends who could readily name both my weaknesses and strengths and were quick to love who I am apart from both. This group prayed for me when I had no more words to do so. They held faith when hope felt scarce. I heard their affirmation and I decided to believe them.

Before we left the table and scattered into our scheduled days, I looked intently at the faces of each of these friends and said, "Thank you. I receive that. I love you."

CHAPTER 10

Joy in Sadness

We shake with joy, we shake with grief.
What a time they have, these two
housed as they are in the same body.

Mary Oliver

MY BODY WAS GREEDY FOR sleep, but it was only two o'clock in the afternoon. I stared blankly out my kitchen window as the golden hours of fall donned their late-day hues. I noticed a cardinal perched on the fence out front that looked a bit like he had slept in his clothes. It appeared as though we might be having similar days. I felt like someone had scooped me out and strewn about my insides, and frankly, I had no energy to retrieve them.

I was up to my elbows in motherhood, grieving the unborn child I lost to miscarriage only the day before and caring for the three-year-old I held in my arms, who very much needed me to have all the usual trimmings of "mom."

This pain—this miscarriage pain—was becoming as familiar to me as the oil stain on my favorite pair of jeans. When a feeling is well known, I think sometimes we expect ourselves to be accustomed to it in a way that will lessen the pain of the injury each time. It's as if we think that taking the element of surprise out of the wound will remove its sting. It doesn't.

You understand. All those relationship breakups don't take the hurt out of the relationship with the one you thought was forever. The many times all of your efforts in finding and interviewing for a job ended in a no doesn't make hearing that disappointing word any easier. Days of parenting a hurting child are the days you know best, but the discouragement remains real and the graces require effort to find.

This particular miscarriage felt different in that it was my first miscarriage since having James. It was equally painful, but it hurt in a different way. Prior to James, the loss was accompanied by the fear that every pregnancy will end in grief and wrestling with the possibility that motherhood wouldn't look anything like I pictured—or happen at all.

Now, with James in my arms, I no longer carry those same fears, but I have a more detailed picture of what I lost. To name just a few things: That feeling of your child being delivered to your ready arms, tender and brand-new. The ongoing wondering of who they look like and what particular gifts God has tucked inside them. The anticipation of watching their personality unfurl before you and getting to know them deeper and differently as they grow in understanding of themselves.

Part of being an adult, I think, is doing the hard work of listening to our feelings and discerning what to do with them. Feelings are real and important. They give us clues about lies we have chosen to believe that may need to be addressed with some truth. They are signs we are paying attention to a broken world and can provide hints to our callings. I have often viewed my feelings as obstacles to push past instead of friends to sit with.

It was Friday, which is traditionally family movie night in our house. I decided to do away with the *night* part and snuggle in with James a little early. I wasn't in the mood to use my feet for anything other than framing the view of my television set. We chose *Inside Out*, one of my personal favorites that James loves too. When your mom is a therapist and your dad works for the Walt Disney Company, *Inside Out* is always on the menu.

I have often viewed my feelings as obstacles to push past instead of friends to sit with.

I hit *play* and collapsed on the couch like a sail cut from the mast, pressing my nose to the back of James's head, kissing him and inhaling his baby scent that lingered through his early years. I just wanted to hold him and take a big drink of him, embracing the simple yet profound truth that he is here. With me.

The Disney Pixar film *Inside Out* is set in the mind of an eleven-year-old midwestern girl named Riley, whose feelings and behaviors are determined by the interplay of five characters that represent her emotions: Joy, Sadness, Anger, Fear, and Disgust.[1] All of these emotions work with and struggle against each other for control and are always impacted by the messages the other four have to share. Yet, it seems apparent as I watch the film that Joy, who is like a blue-haired Tinker Bell without wings, is a bit of an alpha girl: in control and slightly dismissive of the other emotions, especially Sadness. Sadness is (appropriately) colored blue, lethargic, and speaks in a somewhat monotone voice.

Joy struggles to see Sadness's significance and purpose and spends a lot of time just trying to contain her. At one point in the story, when all the other feelings have a role to play, Joy draws a clean, white circle on the floor and instructs Sadness that her job is to stay inside the circle.[2]

But when Riley and her parents move to San Francisco, Joy

struggles to maintain control of the other emotions, especially Sadness. The majority of the movie is a sweet action-packed adventure of Joy and Sadness working together and exploring their relationship with one another.

The relationship between joy and sadness has always been a bit of a conundrum for me in my own life. To embrace both feels like pretending—like drawing silver linings on clouds. Embracing both sadness and joy might require me to say things like, "Everything happens for a reason." Choosing joy feels invalidating to the struggle. Choosing sadness feels like a rejection of hope—denying the truth that the darkness will lift.

This relationship between sadness and joy is an idea I keep returning to, the lock I keep fiddling with. I know God did not orchestrate my suffering, but in His graciousness to me—and to you—He never wastes the pain. I recognize the ways in which heartache has introduced me to hope. I see where growth has sprouted from my grief. I feel grateful for the ways in which pain introduced me to more of God than I knew before. But sadness and joy have felt more like opposites at the end of a spectrum that can never reach each other.

As the movie was nearing its end, James nestled his lanky body closer to me as he anticipated the emotional final scene. James is a deep feeler. I like that about him. The part James was responding to was the scene in which Riley recalled memories of the life she left in the Midwest and missed so much. Sadness was all over that moment, coloring the entire core memory blue. Joy is watching this unfold in dismay, wishing she could rescue the memory by ridding it of sadness altogether. But before she can insert her sunshine, she watches Riley's parents find her, connect with her, and comfort her with a hug in the midst of her sorrow. Instead of shoving Sadness aside as she was accustomed to doing, Joy quietly shares the memory with Sadness. Not one after the other, but together at the same time.[3]

I've met joy in the wake of my sadness—mostly through the

intimacy I've found with God and other people. I've known break-through on the far side of confusing pain. Sadness has been my guide toward connection, grace, and hope. But the presence of joy in the midst of profound grief feels difficult to picture, let alone practice. Jesus shows us a way.

ON THE NIGHT BEFORE JESUS' death, He spent time with His disciples, answering their questions. During this final conversation with them before His death, He encouraged them and shared more truth with His friends. Jesus reminded His friends what it looks like to remain in Him. He prepared them for the reality that many will hate them because of Him. And then He said, "In a little while you will see me no more, and then after a little while you will see me" (John 16:16 NIV). But the disciples' ability to understand the meaning of this statement was limited. Jesus' friends had no category for the pain that was to come and were not able to comprehend a Messiah who would die, rise again, and leave in favor of another counselor, the Holy Spirit.

During this final discourse, the phrase "in a little while" is repeated seven times in just four verses (v.16–19 NIV). This adds to the disciples' anxiety because they don't know what Jesus is referring to, but it is clear that whatever He is speaking of is imminent.[4]

Jesus addressed the disciples' apparent confusion by assuring them that "grief will *turn* to joy" (v. 20 NIV, emphasis added). Jesus was not saying that their pain would be replaced by joy, but would be transformed into joy. To press the point a bit further, Jesus offered the analogy of a woman giving birth. The source of her pain became the very source of her great joy when she held her child in her arms after laboring agony—pain transformed (v. 21).

Years ago, I had the pleasure of working with a young woman who had never known a day without physical pain due to a chronic condition that she was diagnosed with in her early years. She was a senior in college when we worked together, and I learned quickly that her journey had shaped her heart in significant and stunning ways. I cared for her deeply and would have loved to have been able to rescue her from both the emotional and physical pain she experienced. But it was clear to me that she had been a good steward of her pain, letting it shift her perspective and carve strong character within her.

One day I asked her: "How has your pain changed the way you celebrate?"

She smiled and without hesitation said, "I'm just happy to be here."

She elaborated and explained to me that she doesn't fear missing out; she simply feels joy in being present. She's grateful she can dance with her friends, and she feels proud of her strength and what she has accomplished, though the outcome of those achievements may not look as impressive when measured against someone else. "My pain has stolen a lot. But it's given me a lot too," she said. "In fact, in a way, my pain has been the source of a lot of my joy."

This young woman—and many other clients I've been blessed to work with—taught me much about the joy of pain transformed.

YOU HAVE LIKELY EXPERIENCED THIS transformation of pain in your life. Maybe you've sat beside a family member who has been given a difficult diagnosis and told their days are few. While this news remains devastating, your priorities shift, conversations deepen, your relationship is enriched, and possibility expands in the space of numbered days. Perhaps you've trained for a marathon. For months, you've added miles to your training, pushing through fatigue and sore muscles. And when you finally complete the 26.2-mile race, your training becomes your triumph! Or maybe you've experienced a chronic struggle: an autoimmune disease, a hardship in your learning environment, or a relationship that may never be restored. In your hardship, you've learned to see differently, and your loves and values have been rearranged and are now rightly ordered.

What our retrospective view allows us to understand as we consider Jesus' words is that Jesus' death would too become pain transformed. Jesus' death on the cross would be a source of great sorrow and the symbol of the cross would have conjured images of nothing but torture and unfathomable pain. But for Jesus' followers, including you and me, it became something we could boast in—a symbol of the greatest joy we can know. Today, we wear crosses around our necks and place them in our homes as symbols, not of torture but of hope and deep joy. Also, while it felt like despairing news to the disciples that Jesus would no longer be with them, we know that Jesus promised to leave them, and us, with someone greater than Himself: the Holy Spirit. *Pain transformed*.

Jesus doesn't simply tell us that this transformation of pain is possible. He tells us how we can choose joy in the midst of our sorrow (John 16:22). It is worth noting that He does not prescribe a plan that requires us to try harder, work smarter, or be better. He simply tells us to trust three promises.

Jesus' first promise: You will see me again. It's an assurance that makes me weep. You see, this promise not only refers to the resurrection but to Jesus' second coming. You and I will see Him again. Choosing joy is a good idea when we know that what is dark today will not be dark forever, and that I will get to see my Father, which provides hope and joy fit for any circumstance.

Jesus' second promise: You will rejoice. The beauty of this promise is the certainty. Jesus doesn't say we *might* rejoice if our dreams are fulfilled and our circumstances remain comfortable. He doesn't say that rejoicing is our reward if we play our cards right or if we manage to be good enough. He promises that we *will* rejoice.

Jesus' third promise: This joy will not be taken away from you. Not only is joy overflowing—uninhibited by the boundaries and conditions of circumstance—but it is also secure. It will not be snuffed out by a painful event or dynamic in your life. It will not be extinguished by hurt such as disapproval, disappointment, or depression. It will not fade in the light of uncertainty you may be experiencing right now.

Perhaps this is the most distinguishing characteristic of the joy that Christ offers: it extends beyond the boundaries of our circumstances.

This joy is undeniably different from the emotional experience of happiness. In making this comparison, I want to be careful not to minimize the delight that comes from moments of happiness in our lives. These instances of pleasure matter and infuse our lives with beauty and meaning. Sometimes, as Christians, I think we unintentionally make joy the holy version of happy. Said differently, we have vilified *happy* by calling it hedonistic, assuming that earthly pleasures always distract us from God and forgetting that He is the source of this delight too. Or possibly we have decided that happiness is not the hallmark of a mature Christian. But the sensation of happiness should not be relegated to the secular. It's merely a small piece of the joy that is available to us as those who have put our trust in Jesus.

Joy is not a denial of sadness.

Joy is not a denial of sadness. Celebration leaves room for lament as we remember and grieve the loss of something or someone significant and precious to us. Celebration doesn't pretend that pain doesn't hurt. No, celebrating in the midst of our pain means that we allow the sorrowful stories to break our hearts. We let hurt in someone else's story interrupt our own reality. And we celebrate that these stories of pain will not be the last stories told.

I WATCHED JOY AND SADNESS on the screen, feeling the emotion of a scene I'd watched a hundred times. I too am a deep feeler. Most of my favorite memories—the ones I return to again and again and never tire of sharing at dinner parties and during late-night conversations with friends—are held by both sadness and joy. Often the richest celebrations in our lives include both. The wedding of a couple that has done the difficult but worthy work of facing their weaknesses and growing together. A funeral that celebrates the life of someone who has left an indelible mark on the lives of the people who have gathered; they come together to share how they've been changed by the love of the one they lost. The pain makes the joy richer and more nuanced. And the joy transforms the pain by making meaning of it and causing it to become an agent of growth.

Current psychological research also supports the claim that true joy can mingle with sadness and includes but is not limited to the emotional experience of happiness. Professor Sonja Lyubomirsky argues that three classes of factors determine our level of happiness. She says we all have a genetic happiness set point, our genetic dispositions toward happiness, which accounts for 50 percent of our happiness, with circumstances only accounting for about 10 percent, while intentional activities determine about 40 percent of our overall happiness.[5] These are activities and habits that we are empowered to choose in our everyday lives, such as connecting with friends, laughing with your kids, or taking a walk in a picturesque place.

Martin Seligman, known as the founder of modern positive psychology, articulated the PERMA theory of well-being, which says that well-being is based on five main elements:[6]

1. **P**ositive emotion
2. **E**ngagement
3. **R**elationships
4. **M**eaning
5. **A**ccomplishment

It's worth noting that emotion is indeed an element of well-being, but it is just one of five factors. Connection with others in the midst of pain can be a path toward joy. Growth in the wake of grief cultivates joy. Sadness and joy can hold a memory together.

I held James a little tighter, stroking his hair and whispering, "I love you." The credits rolled up the screen and we both continued to stare at the television, neither one of us particularly motivated to move. I asked my three-year-old what he thought the movie meant—a hazard of being the child of a therapist. I imagine I'll hear about this when he's a teenager and that someday he'll roll his eyes and ask me why I can't just enjoy the moment without using every opportunity to insert meaningful conversation. But we're not there yet. I'm not sure what I expected his answer to be, but after a few moments of pause he said, "Sadness helps us find joy." I am equal parts moved and proud. I squeeze my brilliant boy. He's right—and he has no idea he's living proof.

CHAPTER 11

The Dance of Grace

In a very real sense not one of us is qualified, but it seems that God continually chooses the most unqualified to do his work, to bear his glory. If we are qualified, we tend to think that we have done the job ourselves. If we are forced to accept our evident lack of qualification, then there's no danger that we will confuse God's work with our own, or God's glory with our own.

Madeleine L'Engle

AS A CHILD, MY CELEBRATION was uninhibited. Tucked in a childhood photo album in a closet at my parents' house is a photograph of me at three years old, standing in the driveway of the house I grew up in, wearing a faded pink corduroy dress with an enormous Peter Pan collar—a true relic of the early '90s. But the real statement piece and focal point of the photo is a project I had created at preschool: an oversized yellow paper hat with tissue paper in every color you could imagine stuck to it with glue, covering the surface of the hat. When I brought it home, my mom asked if I had left any tissue paper for my classmates to work with. "The black and brown pieces" was my matter-of-fact reply.

The portrait of God's creation and the colors He used to paint it mesmerized the girl in the photograph. God reveals Himself to us in many ways and as a young girl, I saw Him the clearest through the handiwork of His creation. My decision to put my trust in Jesus was born out of a longing to know the artist behind the beauty that shouted His praise in the world around me.

And I shouted back. My joy was exuberant in its expression and I loved with reckless abandon. I can recall snapshots of ordinary moments in my childhood in which I was filled with an inexplicable joy that I now recognize to be the joy of the Holy Spirit. I never put a filter on my feelings or dampened my celebration in response to joy. I saw celebration as a natural response to God's good gifts.

The child in the photograph is a portrait of a girl I hardly recognize.

AFTER MOVING TO CONNECTICUT, I made a habit of being at church every time the doors were open. In the early days of our transition, adjusting to life on the other side of the country, church felt familiar, a safe place. Of course every church is unique and none of them are perfect. But strangers with a shared faith have a difficult time remaining strangers.

When we first began to attend our church, I was asked to be a part of a prayer ministry training—a course that took place once a week on Wednesday nights for eight weeks. During the class, we discussed ways of deepening our prayer life, quieting the mental noise to listen with discernment, as well as protocols on how to best care for congregants who came to us for prayer. It was a rich experience to learn among people who were so passionate about deepening their relationship with God and serving others through prayer.

On a Wednesday evening about midway through the course, we were asked to gather into small groups, taking turns praying for one another and practicing a few of the skills we had learned in the course thus far. I don't recall the specific objective of that night's lesson. But I do remember that one point of caution was that, for many reasons, we were instructed to exercise restraint in making statements of certainty about someone else's life or future such as "You're definitely going to be physically healed!" or "God just told me that you will get engaged next month!"

When it was my turn to share and receive prayer, I decided that the best examples were real examples, and I shared about a job interview I had scheduled for that coming week. The position was, in essence, my dream job: a group private practice with a community of other therapists who were Christians, where I could grow my own business and continue to receive excellent training and support. Being a team member in this group was a coveted position. In anticipation of the interview, I felt insecure and anxious as I wondered about how I was different from all the other candidates who had been given a polite no.

The other group members listened intently and prayed heartfelt prayers for courage, clear thinking, and anointing in the interview, and that the right doors would be opened. When the time of prayer ended, there was a contemplative pause before an older gentleman blurted out, "You are going to get the job!" The group members—especially the leader—cringed as politely as they could. I stared at him, noticing the sincerity of his conviction.

The gentlemen suddenly stood up and announced again, "The job is yours!" flinging his arms in the air in victory like a professional athlete who has just scored the winning goal.

The group facilitator looked outright alarmed. But attempting damage control on his promise at this point would have been like trying to put toothpaste back in the tube. I was hopeful but skeptical. I wouldn't hold this man—or God—to this promise.

It would have made everyone more comfortable if the man in the group had simply stuck to the script. But regardless of the outcome of my interview, I felt grateful for his nerve—the way in which he was willing to celebrate before he knew the answer. Certainly, some may have thought him to be reckless. Admittedly, if I wasn't offered the position, his promise may add to my confusion. But it was more his stance that had me wide-eyed. He was exuberant and uninhibited like it was the most natural response to the situation.

It had been a long time since I had been willing to celebrate like that. The image of the gentleman standing with his arms in a victory *V* ran counter to what I had been taught about what celebration was supposed to look like as Christians. I was a student of many who had implicitly taught me that exuberant celebration was self-aggrandizing. Many of the Christians that I stood shoulder to shoulder with celebrated self-discipline but weren't particularly disciplined about celebration. Over time, I came to understand that celebrating God's good gifts in your own life was inappropriate and would likely hurt other people. So I had become practiced in remaining subdued and keeping my hands to my sides. Celebration became an inside job.

The day of the interview came and while I remained nervous, I was curious about the man's words. The clinical director of the center was running late, leaving me sitting in the waiting room longer than expected. I watched clients arrive, sit, and then follow their therapist out of the lobby. Several therapists passed by on their way to talk with the office manager or check their mailboxes. A half an hour had passed and a man that I presumed to be a therapist on staff walked by me barely taking notice of me on his way to the copier. Copy in hand, he started up the stairs to leave the lobby and then, as if he forgot something, paused, turned around, reentered the waiting room, and proceeded to sit next to me.

"This has never happened to me before, but God very clearly just told me to pray for the woman in the lobby." He paused as if waiting to see if this was, first of all, okay with me, and second, if this made sense to me.

"Well, I'm waiting to interview for a job here so I'll take the prayer!" was my honest reply.

The therapist prayed for me out loud right then, which was wonderful and also made me feel more vulnerable as I was becoming more attached to the idea of working at a place like this.

Regardless of the outcome, I wondered about these two experiences around prayer within a matter of days that seemed so intentional— messages of care cutting through the noise of my own worry about the future. I received these messages not so much as predictions but as provision—assurance that the interview and the job itself (if I was given the opportunity) was less about what I could do and more about what God was already doing.

The interview went well. I felt prepared and conversation came easily with the clinical director. Toward the end of our time together, the director paused, as if debating with himself.

"You're young," he said, pausing, adding to the suspense, "but so was I when I started. Welcome to the center, Nicole."

My experience with the gentlemen's exuberant celebration in the prayer group was challenging my inclination to remain subdued in this moment. Though one could argue I had earned it, it was clear to me that this job was a gift of grace. With this perspective, it was tempting to adopt the mentality "If I didn't earn it, I don't get to celebrate it."

As recipients of grace, we often give ourselves permission to be grateful, but not giddy, as if the discipline of gratitude runs counter to the practice of celebration. As Christians, we often commit to the perspective that exuberant celebration will take us away from God instead of drawing us to Him. We fear that rejoicing will shift the object of our worship to ourselves.

Now I saw my hesitancy to celebrate not as humility but as a sign that actually, I have made my gifts and accomplishments about me.

If celebration is not a symptom of self-absorption, what if a hesitancy to celebrate is?

I recall attending a party several years ago in honor of a friend who had just launched a small business. We had watched her problem-solve, choose perseverance, and use gifts she barely knew she had to launch a business she was passionate about. But instead of relishing the moment with a large group of loved ones who had gathered to cheer for her in this endeavor, she dismissed every congratulatory comment, minimized the accomplishment, and begrudgingly shared several times how unnecessary the celebration was. Because I recognized my friend's struggle inside myself, what was clear to me was that my friend was actually proud of this point of progress but wasn't sure how to appropriately celebrate in that place. She was struggling to reconcile her desire to celebrate with her value of humility.

> *If celebration is not a symptom of self-absorption, what if a hesitancy to celebrate is?*

WHAT IF KNOWING GOD AS the source of our blessing is the very thing that not only gives us the courage to choose joy and celebrate but invites us to be exuberant in our expression? Is this not the heart of worship?

In the Old Testament, King David did not hesitate to be spirited in his expression as the Israelites celebrated the Ark of the Covenant being brought to the city of David. In 2 Samuel 6, we find David leaping and dancing with reckless abandon and oozing with worship. In his celebration, he distributed delicacies to the people, sharing his joy. He was vulnerable as he chose joy, letting his emotions run wild before God and others. Saul's daughter Michal happened to be watching David from her window and she looked upon him with disgust. By her estimation, David's behavior deviated from the dignified manner of a king.

But David's dancing and expressive celebration isn't deviant at all. It's not scandalous conduct that distracts him from God. It's physical worship that connects him to God's love and grace. I find David's response to Michal both simple and profound: David danced because he recognized he had been a recipient of grace. He knew that his position as king was an unearned gift (v. 21). Should we, as recipients of the ultimate grace demonstrated on the cross, not dance all the more? Is there a reason more deserving of our wild celebration than the debt for our sins being paid through Jesus' sacrifice?

Maybe you're like Michal and find yourself disgusted by grand gestures of celebration. Perhaps this expression feels conceited. Maybe you've been told that Christians don't draw attention to their joy. Perhaps you've been taught that we are to be filled with the joy of the Holy Spirit as long as we don't allow our gratitude and awe of God to bubble over in a way that could make others feel uncomfortable. Perhaps you have even elevated certain types of celebration over others. In the name of humility, you've kept your measure of delight small. Or maybe you've refused to celebrate or rejected others' attempts to honor you because you've unknowingly shifted the object of your worship from God to your own achievements. But our hesitancy to celebrate is not a mark of humility but rather a sign that we have made our celebration about ourselves. Possibly your hesitancy to celebrate is a sign that you are celebrating the wrong thing.

I TOO HAVE BEEN A recipient of grace. How could I look at God's good gifts in my life and not express celebration? The girl in the photograph, donning her yellow paper hat, would not have hesitated to dance as a recipient of God's generosity. She would have seen her celebration not as inappropriate but as a natural response to God's goodness in her life. Would I allow the grace I had been given to become my joy too?

I thanked the director and accepted the job on the spot. Arrangements were made and details were discussed before I left the office, walking through the lobby where I had just received prayer and an abundance of God's provision.

I stepped outside the building and let the door slam shut behind me.

And you better believe I threw my hands up in the air in a victory *V*.

CHAPTER 12

Hope in the Middle

> I don't think that anybody can grow unless he really is
> accepted exactly as he is.
>
> Mistor Rogors

"HOW'S IT GOING, SUGAR?" SHE asked. It was Tuesday night, the end of the second day of a four-day marriage intensive. Theta, one of our hosts who has also become a close friend, had spotted me in the corner with my hot tea, pensive.

Theta and her husband, Terry, serve as a host couple for most of the marriage intensives, which means they are responsible for all manner of things related to hospitality. Theta is one of those people whose work reaches far beyond her job description. She anticipates needs and wants before there is a request. She and Terry have both been known to pay attention to someone's favorite candy bar or late-night treat and have it waiting for them before they ask, just to make sure that person feels seen and intentionally loved. Her ears are tuned to God's voice and the nudge of the Holy Spirit is familiar to her. She has been known to wake up in the middle of the night and stay awake to pray for someone without knowing why. But she does it simply because God asks her to and she trusts there's a reason whether she knows that reason or not. Theta and Terry's love and care are essential to the marriage intensive experience. Beyond simply meeting needs, it communicates a message of love and safety and certainly facilitates the work that we do as therapists during our four days together.

I am personally also greatly helped by their ministry.

"Fine," I answered, offering a feeble smile and remembering my friend Elisabeth's definition of that word: an acronym for *feelings inside not expressed*.

Theta patiently waited for the real answer.

"I just want to see breakthrough," I said.

Even after several intensives and thousands of therapy sessions with clients in my private practice, I am still surprised by how working with others' pain gets me all twisted and tangled up in my own. My primary Achilles's heel as a therapist is that I have the tendency to become overly responsible, which leads to me feeling a lot of pressure to perform and, in turn, making therapeutic decisions in an attempt to "fix it." This bad habit is driven by my feelings of inadequacy and rejection—the twin wounds of my life that also show up in my work, uninvited. I'm aware of it. I work on it. I catch myself as often as I can and regulate that pain in order to show up healthy in life and in my therapeutic work, but I miss many opportunities too.

Theta nodded and paused before her eyes met mine. "It's not Thursday yet," she said, referring to the last day of the intensive. She spoke these words with a confidence of a woman who had seen God work wonders.

I knew what Theta was talking about. The statement I make most often when people ask about my experience as a therapist at these intensives is, "I feel like I have a front-row seat to God's miracles."

Frankly, it's astounding to see what God can do in four days or less. It is also astonishing how bone-tired one can be two days in. I give the same encouragement to the couples for whom this intensive experience is brand-new and unlike anything they've ever attended before. My co-therapist, Tim, and I are constantly reminding couples that it is a *four*-day intensive—not a one, two, or three-day intensive. Tim and I find ourselves speaking these words often, especially on Tuesdays. We are speaking to ourselves just as much as we are the couples.

Day two of an intensive is akin to cleaning out a storage closet. It's . . . messy. Pain has been unpacked. There are feelings piled high that have been stuffed in the back corner and gone unlabeled for far too long. Sometimes we find wounds a person didn't know they had, exposed for the first time, and truths that need to be dusted off and put in their proper place. The work is not done and the story is not over. This is what progress looks like on day two.

People often wonder about solutions and what the purpose is in spending so much time understanding pain. Why can't we just move forward with the truth? In order to know what specific truth we personally need to claim, we must understand the pain that we are speaking to. For instance, it is true about you and me that we are valuable. But if you're living your life with the wound that you are powerless, the truth that you are loved will be nice but not particularly helpful to you. In order for the truth to have its way with our wounds, it must be a truth that directly addresses the point of pain.

I hugged Theta, resting my head on her shoulder and soaking in the reality of her reminder. Over her shoulder, I saw a piece of art I had passed a million times in the hallway leading to the snack room. An intensive attendee had created a heart representing each of the four days of the intensive, framed them, and gifted the piece to be hung in the lovely inn to offer hope to couples that would walk the halls after him. The first heart—the Monday heart—is gray like dead tissue, crusted over and cold. The subsequent hearts have more color and signs of life and the final heart—the Thursday heart—is bright red. Not a gory, gross red but more like a celebratory Christmas red. It's shiny and cheerful and you can almost see it pulsing with hope.

"I just wish I could make it better," I whispered. And Theta knew while we might have been talking about the couples, we were also talking about me.

MOST OFTEN, I FIND MYSELF standing squarely in that place—the Tuesday place. It seems I'm never where I want to be or where I feel I should be. I talk with my clients about how *should* is a dangerous word—often a clue that we've believed a lie—damaging messages about what makes us valuable and what keeps us safe. Nevertheless, we flirt with *should* often.

I've noticed that for me the word *should* finds its way into my vocabulary more often at an intensive: I should be the kind of therapist that does the interventions that produce the aha moments and create change by Tuesday. I should be the kind of therapist who is further along in her own healing journey to know better than to hold herself to that kind of standard of perfection. I should be the kind of mom who could never leave her son for four days to show up at these intensives in the first place. I should be the kind of wife who practices the things I preach to the couples all day long during these four days. I should be the person who not only tells others that Jesus is enough and the best prize we could hope for but doesn't feel tempted to add things to Jesus to feel significant and secure myself.

What is perhaps most hurtful beyond these shaming statements is that when I think about my own middle places—those areas in which I see so much room for growth—I struggle to believe I am just as celebrated by my Heavenly Father on Tuesday as I am on Thursday. I find it difficult to spot my value where I currently stand and always picture it on the other side of the growth I hope to see. In other words,

I struggle to embrace all of myself and choose joy in the middle place, between where I've been and where I long to be.

It's worth noting that I see my clients differently and don't hold them to this impossible standard. In fact, when the couples sit down to dinner on the first night, my only goal, to the extent I am empowered to do so, is to make them feel seen and loved, just as they are when they arrive on night one. When I first began working at these intensives I would read the intake forms before I arrived. These forms offer detailed accounts of each person's history, their concerns about the relationship, and their goals for the time they would spend with us. But after a couple of intensives, I decided this strategy was unhelpful. I didn't want to be introduced to the problem before I knew the person. It became important to me to look each person in the eye, share a meal together, and begin to learn his or her story before we unpacked the pain and got down to the business of change. I have also learned that love, not shame, is the best agent of growth.

My high school choral director frequently spoke into this struggle. He was the kind of teacher Hollywood makes movies about. A talented musician and choral director, I'm confident he could have held other more prestigious positions at a more impressive institution. But he felt God's call to hold his post at our small K–12 school. He was invested in our personal process and not simply outcomes. Many rehearsals came and went without us ever singing a note because he had something important to tell us about Jesus and His love that just couldn't wait.

A statement he shared frequently that became the anthem of my high school years is "Love where you are and grow from there." He desperately wanted us to know that while as a teenager, and any age really, we have ample room for growth, and we are just as loved as we ever will be in that place. Though I felt assured by those words then and through the years, I've struggled to trust their truth.

I've wrestled with the idea that celebration and growth can coexist.

On the one hand, recognizing areas in which I need to mature suggests that I need to make progress in those areas before I allow myself to celebrate, turning celebration into an earned reward. On the other hand, I fear that celebrating that I am valued where I stand now with much room for improvement will make me complacent in my desire to grow. I wonder if in some ways, I (and maybe you too) have equated celebration with endings rather than points of progress. I suspect that I have limited celebration to my own success instead of marveling at the work of God along the way or having a posture of curiosity and excitement when I can't yet see what He is doing.

Theta's reminder that Thursday was yet to come was twofold. Most obviously, it meant that the intensive was only halfway through and there was more work to be done. But her words were also meant to remind me of what the ending looked like.

The four-day experience ends on Thursday afternoon at the cross on a hill overlooking the property. Walking with these couples that have been bold in sharing their stories and brave to let God do His healing work in them is a gift I'll never get over. To be clear, each couple arrives at the cross differently. Some couples have encountered the miracle they've prayed for. For some, this time represents an ending—the relinquishing of a stronghold they are committed to no longer carrying with them. For many, this time represents a new beginning—the start of learning to walk in a new way.

Joy feels scary in the absence of certainty. We feel safer knowing that all is well in the end before we walk through the middle, wrought with unknowns and the possibility of disappointment. What if we give the relationship our best effort and it isn't restored? What if we take a chance on hope, only to be heartbroken in the end? What if I try my best and I still fail? What if we are brave enough to dream, and the reality doesn't match the dream?

It is difficult to hold joy and celebrate God's promises before we know the outcome of these assurances in our own lives. I find it vulnerable to lean into courage in the middle when I haven't read the end of the story. Perhaps, like me, you are in a season in which it is easier for the feelings to feel stronger than the faith. Walking forward with what we know to be true in spite of how we feel is terrifying.

But when I consider the cross, I remember that no matter how messy our middles look, or how hurt our hearts might be in the midst of our growth, we already know the ending.

Those who have put their trust in Jesus have assurance that in the midst of uncertainty, our future is sure. If your personal experience was the only truth you knew, choosing joy would be a gamble at best. But it's not all you have. You and I both know how this story ends. Unlike the disciples who grieved Jesus' death on Friday and who mourned in hopeless anguish on Saturday with no promise of Sunday, we can sit in the midst of our in between places and celebrate the joy of what happened on the third day—and what will happen on the last day when Jesus returns once again. Jesus' death and resurrection invites us to rest assured that the darkness will lift. We get to feel joy in the fact that what we can see from where we stand right now is not a complete view.

JOB, WHO IS DESCRIBED AS a man of honor who walked closely with God, was familiar with the middle place. The Bible tells us that Satan taunted God, claiming that if he persecuted Job enough times in enough ways, Job would turn his back on God. But God knew that Job was faithful and this story proved to be true. Job endured great suffering, including physical pain, the loss of loved ones, and feeling betrayed by his friends.

We are privy to several conversations between God and Job. Job is honest about his disappointment and despair surrounding his circumstances. He speaks frankly about his feelings toward God and the people in his life. And God speaks directly in return. The thread throughout their dialogue is God reminding Job of who He is and who Job is in relation to God. Job's pain persisted and he sat in his pit of suffering and sorrow, holding more questions than answers. But remembering who God was and who He was in Job's middle place helped him remain confident of the hopeful end when he claimed, "For I know that my Redeemer lives, and at the last he will stand upon the earth" (Job 19:25 ESV). In Job's confusion and devastation, he stands upon the secure truth that Christ will stand upon the earth, defeating darkness. In the middle of his suffering with no solution, Job celebrates his Savior. Authentic celebration is possible not when we fully comprehend our circumstances but when we rightly know God and recognize His authority.

You may feel like me on a Tuesday right now. The mess has been unpacked, and you can't find the hope under the piles of heartache, longing, betrayal, disappointment, and loneliness to name just a few items. Maybe you're praying for a child to make different choices and you're wondering if he or she will ever want wholeness. Perhaps singleness has defined this chapter of your life. You've found fulfillment, but you feel ready to turn the page and share your life with someone. Possibly you've waded through significant trauma. You've found significant healing but properly processing the pain is a reality you wrestle with daily.

What I want to say to you are the words that Theta shared with me: It's not Thursday yet. I'd love to be with you right here, right now, sitting at the foot of the cross together, shoulder to shoulder, you and me. We bring different stories to this place. We carry different wounds to the cross that held our wounded Healer. The ground is level here at the foot of the cross. We stand in our middle places, equally in need of rescue. Together, I want to remember that because Jesus absorbed the pain of our humanity on the cross, you and I can celebrate right now. The ending is all the hope we need for the middle—the Tuesday seasons of our lives.

Personally, I am not yet where I hope I will be someday. I hope that with more wrinkles, I become wiser. I pray that as time passes, I continue to grow in grace and walk deeper into my faith and in my relationships with myself and others. From where I stand, I see ample room for improvement. And yet, I celebrate with gratitude for what God has done and the ways He continues to work in my heart—and in yours. We can love where we are and want more for ourselves at the same time.

Sometimes the miracle is movement we absolutely cannot see from where we sit in the middle place. Often, the answer to a prayer looks like an answer we didn't know to pray for. But every moment—especially on the Tuesdays—offers an opportunity to celebrate that God is who He says He is and He can do what He says He can do, even before the story is finished. Celebrating the end is our hope and joy for the middle.

Celebrating the end is our hope and joy for the middle.

I went to bed that night at the retreat weary from the first two days. I settled in to rest with all the loose ends of more therapeutic work to be done and more aware than ever of my own weaknesses, both as a therapist and a person. I snuggled into bed, under the weight of hand-stitched quilts, and felt held by the promise that the best is always yet to come. I texted my husband at home in Connecticut, feeling the tension of the calling to be here and the longing to be there at the same time. I closed my eyes that stung from dryness and were ready for sleep. And the only prayer I had the energy to whisper on that Tuesday night was "Thank you for Thursday."

CHAPTER 13

Joining Others' Joy

Joy is a net of love in which you can catch souls.

Mother Teresa

I NEVER THOUGHT I WOULD have a son. I was sure that if Jimmy and I were blessed with children, they would be girls—not necessarily because this is what I wanted, but because girls were what I knew. I am the oldest of three daughters, we have a goddaughter who stole our hearts from her first breath, and it was easy for me to picture tea parties, baby dolls, and all things pink in our home. When I learned that our second miracle baby—Charlie—was also a boy, I was equal parts thrilled and terrified by what I didn't know about raising boys.

We are learning together, James, Charlie, and I. We are learning the same way you learn anything: fits and starts, mistakes and repair, grace and growth.

My little boys have each brought so much wonder to my life. When I tiptoe into James's room late at night to pull the covers back over his slack body, I marvel at his cherub-like face—his blonde hair sweaty and stuck to his forehead and Lightning McQueen flashing behind his eyelids in his dreams. Often, I slip into Charlie's room before going to bed myself just to watch him sleep—the rhythmic rise and fall of his chest through the wooden slats of his crib is a view that will never fade into the background for me. The news that I was pregnant with Charlie came when I'd nearly walked out on hope of having more children. Both of my boys were God's kindness to us.

Still, being a mom of boys was a slough of new experiences. I learned quickly that there is no physical pain quite like stepping on a Lego with your bare feet. And despite James's extensive vocabulary for a young boy, the soundtrack of my days were mostly a series of sound effects: *Boom! Ping! Grrrrr!*

Now, with James nearly five years old, I was fascinated by his evolving deep passions. His first obsession (and first word) was buses, which moved naturally into trucks of all varieties but mostly construction trucks. He had a brief interest in sea creatures. And James's love for the color green has been a through line in all of these stages.

His strongest and most enduring phase, however, has been his passion for mysteries and detective work. He has a detective hat and dark glasses with "rearview mirrors" so he can see behind him without turning his head, which are only partially effective. He takes his work with his fingerprinting kit very seriously and is much more motivated to practice his letters and numbers if he can write a secret code. And on several occasions Jimmy and I have had to remind him that his friends might not appreciate being arrested every time he sees them. Aiding his imagination, James loves The Hardy Boys series from decades ago. He inherited, or more likely was influenced by, my love for mysteries and we both look forward to being transported to the lives of young detectives from the 1950s.

But there was one passion that often comes with being a mother of boys that I swore I would never accept: Nerf guns. I knew plenty of wholesome families whose kids played with Nerf guns. I babysat several boys growing up who played with them and were boys I would consider to be role models for my sons. Still, I couldn't get over the "gun" part of Nerf guns despite their friendly neon colors and soft foam darts—darts that somehow manage to find their way into every corner of your house from your ceiling fan to your underwear drawer.

But on a Wednesday afternoon at the park, a herd of elementary school boys migrated through the playground where we chose to spend our afternoon and onto our neighborhood beach. Ducking behind stone walls, swooping down plastic playground slides, and darting out from under lifeguard towers, we found ourselves in the center of a battle and it was a blast. There was absolutely nothing violent about this war, just belly laughs, staccato sound effects, and cheering—a glimpse of what childhood should be and rarely is anymore. The expression of awe on James's face melted whatever stubbornness was left in me.

A week before James's birthday, Jimmy and I were sitting on the couch when I swallowed my pride and staring straight head, whispered, "I think we should get James a Nerf gun."

I tossed the idea out offhandedly and Jimmy caught it equally casually, playing along. He simply nodded and reached across the couch to hold my hand. He knew I just needed a few years to warm up to the idea.

"Actually two," I clarified. "One for him and one for a friend . . . or me. You know, so we can have Nerf wars," I said as nonchalantly as I could manage.

James's birthday arrived and we celebrated with all of our usual traditions. Five green streamers—one for each year—were taped across the stairs for James to break through in the morning as he came downstairs, a tradition adopted from my friend Elisabeth and her family. James enjoyed a breakfast on the red "You Are Special Today" plate. Jimmy had worked his meticulous magic with a can of Granny Smith

Apple green spray paint and a bed sheet to make a large sign that read "Happy 5th Birthday James Z" to hang on the fence that borders the village green, down the street from our house—a birthday tradition for the kids and the "kids at heart" in our neighborhood. His grandparents had gifted James tokens for ice cream at Brendan's 101, the local ice cream and sandwich shop, and we walked down the street for a midday treat, debating the ice cream flavor choices of East Beach Heath or McKinley Mint. And in the evening James opened his gifts, wrapped in brown paper and tied with green satin ribbon—among them, the two Nerf guns. His celebratory dance and smile of contentment had me wondering if there was some sort of hall of fame for mothers like me.

Now, when we finish dinner early with time to spare before bedtime, we look at each other and smile and ask, "Nerf war?" We race up the stairs because while I have grown and evolved as a mother of sons, I have my limits and have made a rule of confining the small foam darts to our play space. We dive behind couches and use pillows as shields and yell and cheer and laugh so hard that we lose our aim.

Sometimes loving others asks us to celebrate what they love, even if it feels unfamiliar to us.

Sometimes loving others asks us to celebrate what they love, even if it feels unfamiliar to us.

Celebrating others should never require us to compromise our values. But celebration will ask us to step beyond our own proclivities and preferences to join our loved ones in their passions and to share in the excitement over what matters most to them.

One of the gifts of relationships is that they allow us to experience joy we may not encounter on our own. Left with an empty afternoon, you will not find me running about my house with a Nerf gun in hand. I, as Nicole, still don't prefer Nerf guns. But I, as the mom to James, love them. I find such a thrill in being doubled over in laughter with my boy. I appreciate the way it forces my responsibilities to scoot over and make some room for fun—fun that I might consider unnecessary if it weren't for James's presence reminding me otherwise.

Relationships will cost you time, energy, creativity, and money that you might spend differently if it were just you. You might feel awkward and uncomfortable as you learn to love the things that matter to someone else. But celebrating others sacrificially is never wasted effort.

THE CALL TO HONOR OTHERS is consistent throughout the Bible. I am inspired by the apostle Paul's letter to the Romans when he includes honor in his instruction for believers to love one another. At the time Paul wrote this letter, the Jews and Gentiles were at odds with each other. The call Paul gave to "honor one another above yourselves" (Romans 12:10 NIV) is also translated "in honor giving preference to one another" (NKJV) and was intended to lead to unity. Paul pressed his audience beyond asking them to simply have affection for one another by instructing them to celebrate their fellow Christ-followers by putting the other's desires first.

Celebrating others by honoring them might mean being willing to accelerate their dreams by making a connection between friends who have opportunities and wisdom to offer each other or using whatever platform you've been given to share someone else's message and ask others to join you on stages to which you've been invited.

Or maybe you have a friend with whom you share little in common. What if you saw the space between her interests and yours as an opportunity to learn something new?

Maybe you often find yourself feeling frustrated by the way your spouse expresses love and often feel resentful that he or she just isn't loving you the "right" way. What if your irritation became your invitation to go first, to be the pursuer of the connection you long to have?

Perhaps every question you ask your teenager is met with a blank expression and one-word answers. What if that facial expression became your cue to ask your child to educate you about something that matters to him—even if it is a hobby that's of no interest to you or that action movie you can barely tolerate.

For several years I worked with a delightful couple in my counseling practice. Sometimes people come to counseling in crisis or with a specific issue to address. Other times, individuals or couples seek my services simply out of a desire for growth or deeper understanding and intimacy with one another. This particular couple fell into the latter category.

The husband was passionate about golf and often connected with friends and spent his days off work on the golf course. His wife did not share his love for golf. It wasn't a point of contention, but she never had an interest in learning and they both felt fine about that activity being "his." "It's just not my thing," she would often say.

During one session, after several months of working together, both of them entered my office very obviously excited. They sat down on my couch and were eager to share with me what had happened over the weekend. The weather was exceptionally warm for April and the husband had asked his wife to ride along with him in the golf cart so they could enjoy the day together. He reported being a little surprised when she readily agreed. They both grinned like Cheshire cats as they told me about how she asked him if she could take a shot too. "Of course!" he had said. But he was shocked when she took her driver and with near-perfect form sent the ball sailing down the fairway, landing inches from the hole. Unbeknownst to her husband, she had been taking lessons for months, waiting for the perfect opportunity to surprise him, knowing how much it would mean to her husband to join him in his passion.

"I still don't really love golf," she said. "But I love golf together."

THE APOSTLE PAUL CONTINUED HIS instruction on how to actively love one another by giving the famous command, "Rejoice with those who rejoice; mourn with those who mourn" (Romans 12:15 NIV). To mourn with those who mourn means allowing someone else's grief to take up space in your heart. It requires letting your routines be interrupted by someone else's reality. Rejoicing with those who rejoice often looks like participating in the activity or interest that causes our loved ones to rejoice and celebrating others' joy, even if it's a joy you wish was your own. This is not a passive form of love but an active one. Paul is asking you and me to push past our own preferences and step off the sidelines of other people's joy and join them—regardless of how closely your joy matches their joy.

We often talk about how differences and disagreements between us as human beings are agents of personal development. We discuss how we are sharpened when confronted with people who see the world differently than we do or simply find someone's personality difficult to love. But the discipline of participating in others' celebration will also significantly shape us.

Every time I find a foam dart in my shoe, I think about the privilege of participating in James's joy—thankful for the avenue of connection paved by celebration. Every time I miss the target altogether because the two of us are laughing too hard to see straight, I feel grateful for the many ways God will teach me something new and important through the gift of being his mom. I am aware that I will be sharpened through the challenge of motherhood. But I also praise God for the invitation to grow through learning to celebrate what others love—even if celebration looks like refining my battle strategy for a Nerf war.

PART III

FIND THE COURAGE
TO CELEBRATE

CHAPTER 14

Keep the Thank-You Notes

I would maintain that thanks are the highest form of thought; and that gratitude is happiness doubled by wonder.

G.K. Chesterton

DURING A TRIP TO PASADENA, Jimmy and I visited our friends Terry and Sharon at their home for dinner. It had been several years since we moved from California to Connecticut, but their house would always feel like a safe harbor. Many memorable conversations happened around their dining room table, on their living room couches, or on the back patio of that house. Both Terry and Sharon claimed that they were not exceptionally gifted in hospitality, but every encounter I had with them made a strong argument against this assertion. They didn't simply practice hospitality; they embodied it . . .

On the menu that evening was beef Bourguignon—a dish I've never felt brave enough to attempt myself but thoroughly enjoyed.

The four of us filled one another in on the details of our lives—particulars that sometimes get lost in the distance between California and Connecticut. We reminisced, telling stories we had all heard several times before but would never tire of remembering and retelling. I loved learning from Terry and Sharon and felt grateful that our friendship had wandered beyond the limits of graduate school.

I met Terry as a graduate student at Fuller. I realized therapy was an art form the first time I witnessed Terry's therapeutic work and asked if he would be willing to train me outside of our regularly scheduled courses. He graciously agreed and has continued to consult with me over the last decade. And the more time I spent learning about counseling under his leadership, the more I wanted to do life like him too. Terry and Sharon's personal care and their work have shaped the way I see the world and the events and relationships within it.

About midway through the meal, I slid a note I had written Terry across the dining table and placed it in his hands. Training with him—even in different time zones and with many states between us—had been transformational in both my work and personal growth, and one of the most generous, most valuable gifts I had been given in my life. I needed him to know that.

In the note, I wrote that the experience of being his student felt more like discipleship than simply learning or training. I shared that what I had learned recently about discipleship is that in biblical times, a disciple wasn't just somebody who wanted to know the information the Rabbi knew but someone who also sought to emulate the Rabbi's actions—to become like the Rabbi. There was even an idea that as a disciple, you would follow the Rabbi so closely that you would be covered in your Rabbi's dust, both literally and figuratively.[1] In my note, I told him that one of the characteristics I valued most about his teaching and training is that he continually turns me toward Christ. As for teachers I've encountered in this life, there's no one's dust I would rather be covered in than his.

I continued the letter by saying that I am far from a perfect therapist—or the clinician I hope I will be someday. But because of his guidance, I know exactly what it looks like to be a wise therapist. I shared that his work has taught me how to see people—their victories and limitations—in the context of his or her story. He has shown me how to look beyond the dialogue in a relationship to hear the painful and peaceful dynamics between individuals. I told him that his mentorship has influenced my own growth, my work, my marriage, and my parenting. He is an example of what it looks like to live generously—that a life poured out for others will always be a life well spent. I thanked him for his investment in me as a person as well as my therapeutic work and for teaching me to be a good steward of my pain. I wrote that his mentorship is evidence of God's lavish love and one of the best gifts I have ever received. I ended the note by saying, "I am very blessed to be covered in your dust."

Terry looked up from the note, his face communicating everything he couldn't say with his words in that moment. "Thank you so much," he said. And then finally asked, "Why now?"

"I just really wanted you to know," I said.

I hoped the thank-you note would bless him, but I grossly underestimated the gift that sharing my thankfulness in his presence would give to me. Gratitude will always breed joy. But the experience of feeling grateful, articulating that gratitude, and sharing it with that person directly extends the boundaries of our joy and expands our capacity for celebration.

I AM REMINDED OF THE story from Luke 17:11–19 about the ten lepers who cried out to Jesus for healing. Because Jesus was on the border of Samaria and Galilee, we can assume this was an ethnically mixed group of men. A Samaritan, while part Jewish, was hated by Jews and often cast aside. Their shared misery brought this unlikely group together. One commentator says, "Their common affliction of these men has erased their ethnic differences."[2] Their identity as outcasts of society was stronger than their cultural or religious affiliations. They were human beings with feelings and opinions, gifts and talents, but their disease defined their identity as they were forced to shout "Unclean! Unclean!" as they hobbled through the streets (Leviticus 13:45 NIV). Leprosy was believed to be a sign of God's judgment, which solicited less compassion, and it was assumed that the lepers brought their condition on themselves.[3] From their place at the bottom of society (especially the Samaritan), they had nothing left to lose in shouting something different to Jesus when they caught sight of Him.

"Have mercy on us!" they cried (v. 13 ESV). As a God who sees our pain, Jesus saw them and had compassion on them and instructed the group to go to see the priest, which is traditionally what one did after having been healed.[4] In essence, Jesus was telling them to have faith that they would be cured. As is the case with many stories in scripture, the healing would follow obedience.

The entire group made their way toward the temple, and on their way they recognized their own healing in their friends. Faces were restored to their original form, body parts were repaired, and their skin became smooth and blemish free, and therefore, their social and religious health was instantly restored.

All ten men demonstrated their faith and were physically cured. All ten men celebrated the outcome of their ask. All ten men felt grateful. But only the Samaritan returned to thank Jesus and praise God for his healing. The other nine men celebrated their physical healing and returned to a life of ethnic separation and distinction. But the Samaritan returned to Jesus—a Jew—threw himself at Jesus' feet, thanked Him, and gave glory to God. One commentator notes that the language of "'seeing' . . . 'returning' . . . and 'glorifying God'" echoes the shepherds' response to the angelic announcement of Christ's birth and their visit to the manger.[5] The Samaritan's distinctive way of "seeing" elicits praise and celebration.

In returning to Jesus, we can assume that the Samaritan not only celebrates his physical healing but that his bodily restoration is also an inwardly transformative experience for him. The Samaritan sees Jesus as not simply his Healer but also his Hope.

Jesus responded by asking about the other nine. "Were not all ten healed?" (v. 17 THE MESSAGE). And turning to the Samaritan, He said, "Your faith has healed and saved you" (v. 19 THE MESSAGE). The ten lepers' obedience had cured them physically. But the Samaritan's faith had made him well in body and soul. Giving glory to God had made him whole and took his healing beyond the boundaries of his body to include a spiritual healing.

EVERY TIME I'VE HEARD THIS story, I've sincerely believed that I would be the one—the Samaritan whose gratitude and celebration propelled him to glorify God. How could nine out of the ten men neglect to say a simple thank you? Now, I recognize that too often I can be found standing among the other nine.

The other nine men were undoubtedly physically and emotionally relieved and felt grateful for their healing. After being rejected and isolated for a long period of time, I know I would feel eager to reengage with my loved ones and reenter society.

We might be tempted to judge the other nine men who felt grateful but did not return to thank Jesus. But how often do we as recipients of God's good gifts celebrate the outcome—physical healing, a relationship restored, emotional growth—and feel genuine gratitude without giving credit to God and thanking Him for what He has done? Can we recognize that in our relief, we often fail to remember the source of our restoration? Are we willing to be transformed and see Jesus as not only our Healer, but also our only Hope?

Often, I assume that my inward emotional experience of gratitude offers the same benefit as outwardly expressing my appreciation to God through the practice of thanksgiving. But Jesus clearly distinguishes the difference between the two in His conversation with the Samaritan. Thanksgiving is the expression of the gratitude we feel.

Surely our God who is aware of our motives and actions and understands and perceives our thoughts and feelings knows of the gratitude we carry in our hearts. But Jesus' insistence on thanksgiving is not merely a bid for our praise. It's an invitation to connect with Him—in our joy. Practicing thanksgiving reminds us that gifts always come from outside ourselves. And perhaps most importantly, thanksgiving bonds us with God—the source of all joy.

Celebrating good news is a grace. But what a treasure we have in the invitation to celebrate with our heavenly Father through thanksgiving. The practice of thanksgiving reminds us that God is not only present in our pain but also present at the party. God is near and His touch is tender as He walks with us over the uneven plains of longing and uncertainty and across the perilous terrain of heartbreak and sorrow. But when we reach ground that is soft underfoot—seasons characterized by breakthrough and good news—He does not let go. Our God is not only available to us in our struggle but also longs to join us in our joy.

> *The practice of thanksgiving reminds us that God is not only present in our pain but also present at the party.*

It's likely that if you glanced around at your life for a moment, you could tell me about several people, moments of glee and delight, and blessings that have brought you joy. Maybe your gratitude for these gifts has led you to express thanksgiving. But if like me you are prone to settle for feeling grateful, aren't you just a little bit curious about what you might be missing out on in your relationship with Jesus by not sharing in your joy with Him?

Years ago, I had the pleasure of working with a couple who sought therapy for help in recovering from a betrayal. After months of dedicated work on both individuals' parts, love and trust were beginning to be reestablished and restored. We had worked consistently together for almost a year when the husband sat down on my couch and announced immediately to me and his wife that he had something he wanted to say before our hour together progressed. Naturally, I felt both curious and a little uneasy. I was encouraged by the progress we had made, but the strong bond between the two of them still felt new and tenuous. However, my training had taught me to use whatever feeling and relationship dynamic is in the room at the moment, so I was confident that his words—whatever they were—would offer therapeutic opportunity. Still, I was surprised when the husband turned to face the wife and said, "I just want to say thank you."

The woman smiled—equally surprised—and asked, "For what?"

He was ready with an answer. "I could thank you for everything you do to serve our family, and I am thankful for those things." The strength of his voice faded as tears were beckoned forth. "What I really want to say is, thank you for choosing me and for fighting for us."

The practice of thanksgiving forged a connection between the two of them that was beyond my reach as a therapist in that moment—connection that would have been difficult to deepen had the man simply felt gratitude in his heart.

Jesus' instruction as well as the joy I witnessed from the couch in my office is more than sentimentality. Current research confirms that gratitude is more than an attitude or posture. Fully experiencing the benefits of gratitude requires action. Clinician and professor Alan Carr says that, "Gratitude involves recalling these gifts, appreciating their benefits, experiencing positive emotions and expressing this appreciation by showing that we are thankful and generously giving gifts to others."[6] Certainly gratitude includes noticing, appreciating, and celebrating the goodness we see in our lives. But expression of that appreciation and active generosity are also essential to deepening our joy and connection with others.

Also, actually speaking our thankfulness in our everyday conversations with ourselves and others makes an important difference in our ability to experience gratitude's full effects.[7]

Martin Seligman also found the expression and interpersonal component of gratitude to be beneficial. In a study he conducted, he concluded that writing a gratitude letter, visiting the person to whom it was written and reading it to them out loud had a positive effect on well-being.[8] In the letters, people described how they had been helped, the impact this help had on them personally, and how thankful they felt. Seligman's study serves as further evidence that our thank-yous connect us with others—God and the people in our community—in our celebration.

This relational bond is just one of many ways gratitude improves our sense of well-being. Thanksgiving broadens our vision to see more possibilities. What a difference it would make if when confronted with obstacles, you and I were more inclined to consider what is possible instead of being encumbered by the problem. What would it be like to dream about the future and actually feel excited about all the ways God could move rather than choosing to practice disappointment and rehearse disaster?

Also, thanksgiving will prevent us from taking goodness for granted and reminds us to savor the moment. Thankfulness refuses to allow present gifts to go stale. It feels foreign to imagine the joy of a new relationship, a newborn, or the start of your dream job going stale. But when the quirks turn to annoyances, the sleepless nights come, and the inevitable imperfections of your work reveal themselves, we can quickly turn even the most beloved blessing into a burden. Perhaps you're thinking of another treasured gift in your life—an opportunity or person that you swore you'd never take for granted. But as the novelty wears off and what is precious to you finds its place in the ordinary cadence of your days, discontentment moves in, and others' faults become far too easy to find.

What I find most helpful is that thanksgiving keeps our eyes trained on what is good instead of what is wrong, which includes how we see and think about others and ourselves. What if you performed a task, gave a speech, led a discussion or event and didn't immediately recount the mistakes you made and chide yourself for all the things you could have done differently? What if you received a compliment and considered its truth rather than instantly dismissing its validity? How might you feel differently if you gave thanks for the goodness you unwrapped through the hours of a day, rather than dwelling on everything that didn't happen? What would it be like to be brave enough to acknowledge the strengths you bring to a group, instead of merely being willing to evaluate your weaknesses?

Imagine the view we would see of others through the lens of thankfulness! How would it change our relationships if we appreciated what others add to our lives, instead of being frustrated and resentful about what they lack? How might we move from judgment to joy if we focused on others' good qualities? How would our perspective shift if we stopped wishing our friends and family members were a little more like us and noticed with awe and wonder the ways that they were created uniquely and think differently than we do instead?

And what might you and I be missing in our relationship with Jesus if we stop short at feeling grateful instead of being thankful? If thanksgiving is an avenue we've been given to celebrate with our heavenly Father—the God who holds us in both our pain and our joy—how can we not lift our hands in praise?

WE LAID DOWN OUR FORKS in surrender to the empty plates and our hands wrapped around piping-hot cups of tea. Terry's tea selection was more like a tea collection and a bit of a ritual in my conversations and training with him.

Sharon smiled from her seat at the end of the table and said, "You know, I've often told Terry that he should keep the thank-you notes he receives from students over the years. They are so meaningful and should be treasured—saved for days when the truth is more challenging to remember."

There was a hum of agreement around the table—each of us reflecting on how helpful it is to return to the stories that remind us of our significance and sense of security in the world. In noticing, appreciating, articulating, and telling these stories of thanksgiving, we are building something worthy and enduring.

Don't wait. Live your thanksgiving stories. Write your thanksgiving down. And tell those tales with gratitude again and again. These are the stories we need to hear often—the ones that are worth retelling around the dinner table, bonfires, and when it's past someone's bedtime.

And when you are on the receiving end of these tales of thanksgiving, save them. Savor them. Keep the thank-you notes.

"Keep the thank-you notes" is a phrase we now rely on to cue us to remember the truth, to notice what is right and good, and to build a foundation of connection with God and with the people inside and outside our home. One note, one story of thanksgiving at a time, we are creating a culture of celebration.

CHAPTER 15

Practice Savoring

Grant us joy and make our song Alleluia . . . not because we
aren't paying attention, but because we are.

Nadia Bolz-Weber

THE FACT THAT I WAS born and raised in Seattle is fundamental to who
I am. When people ask me to describe myself, I always mention that
I am from the Pacific Northwest first. It feels important that people
know that about me. I spent my college and graduate school years in
California. I currently live in Connecticut and even call it "home." But
though Connecticut is home, I will always be from Seattle. I am at my
core a West Coast girl. I notice my Pacific Northwest upbringing in
the kind of things I find beautiful: evergreen winters, mountains that
look like the top of a vanilla ice cream cone, tulips that dot the land-
scape each May. I notice it in the way I prefer to connect with others:
cozy gatherings, snuggled under fleece blankets at the end of a dock
or on the bow of a boat, or huddled by the fireplace in the corner of

a coffee shop. Coffee isn't simply something that Seattleites enjoy; it's part of the culture. Many business deals, relationship milestones, and pivotal decisions are made over a cappuccino or a Gibraltar.

When I think about who was there in my childhood—those who witnessed my struggles and wins, encouraged my faith, prayed me through pivotal seasons, and loved me through my Meg Ryan haircut at age fourteen—the Bible study my parents were a part of is there. I know what people are referring to when they say that it takes a village to raise a child because in addition to a few other key families in my childhood, this was my village growing up. My parents met with the same group of people for over twenty-five years and many of their kids were some of my dearest friends and felt like the older siblings I never had.

ONE SUMMER EVENING DURING A trip to visit my family in Seattle, my parents invited the families in their Bible study over for dinner on their back patio. The gathering in my parents' backyard was quintessential Seattle. The daylight stretched until nearly 10:00 p.m. and we huddled under navy blue fleece blankets in the evening chill. We enjoyed second and third helpings of grilled salmon, spinach salad, and crab cakes. For some of these friends, years had passed since I last hugged them. But the conversation was easy and familiar, as if we'd been with each other the whole time. I watched them pass baby Charlie around the table—a baby this group had faithfully prayed for from the other side of the country. And beyond the patio, I delighted in watching members of the group love on James as they had loved me at his age—letting him win game after game of corn hole and holding his hand to walk up and down the dock as many times as he wished.

Around the table, we talked about everything from our most treasured dreams in this season to the unseasonably warm weather.

As we transitioned from dinner to dessert—my mom's famous chocolate chip cookies—we started playing dominoes, asking and answering questions about what was good and what was hard about our lives in this season over the clinking of the domino tiles on the glass table. The tone of the time felt both lighthearted and deeply meaningful. In the presence of this group, it felt just a little bit easier to remember what matters most in life: a relationship with God and companionship with the people He brings alongside us in our journey. I've lived enough years with this group as characters in my everyday life to know them as priceless treasures. And I've lived enough of my life without them nearby to know that not everyone is blessed with a community like this one.

One thing I notice about myself in the context of the Bible study group is that I laugh easily. Left on neutral, I lean a little serious. But I am thankful for the grace of having an easy laugh, and with this group, I laugh loud and often—one of the simplest, yet most profound means of celebration we can practice, I think.

The moon rose, spotlighting the lake. Tealight candles danced in glass votives on the table. I felt full and satisfied in a way that made me want to memorize every detail of this moment—to somehow capture what I knew I could not keep. Yes, the relationships would stretch beyond the evening. The truths we remembered together would endure. But it felt important to savor *this* memory—to not only appreciate what these people have meant to my life across the years but to celebrate by marking this moment as noteworthy and special.

Savoring is subtle but significant celebration.

Savoring is subtle but significant celebration. It expands and deepens the seemingly ordinary events of our daily lives. Savoring moves us from knowing God's goodness to encountering it and basking in it. To practice savoring requires noticing, naming, valuing, and expressing gratitude for the experience, making deeper meaning of the memory, and helping the emotional experience last longer so that it can also be recalled later.[1]

When you flip through the archives of your memories, you'll come across some seemingly insignificant images or experiences: the contentment you felt in licking that ice cream cone on your vacation at the beach, the tender touch of your toddler's hand in your own as you made the slow and tentative walk down the hallway of the house, the look on your best friend's face as you talked with her over coffee for longer than you planned on that Wednesday afternoon. Savoring writes the memory in permanent ink where your brain might be tempted to discard it as inconsequential. Savoring celebrates the ordinary.

GOD INVITES US TO CELEBRATE His goodness and enjoy His gifts through the psalmist's words, "Taste and see that the LORD is good" (Psalm 34:8 NIV). The fact that two of the five traditional senses are mentioned here is no mistake or coincidence. One thing I have discovered is that God made us to be experiential learners. Insight is helpful and certainly important as we seek to understand a problem and move toward growth. But often, we need to experience something new in order to change our thinking or adopt a new action pattern. Knowing the warmth of God's joy means not just knowing it exists but participating in this joy ourselves through the practice of savoring.

Savoring requires that we regard the moment we are living in as more important than anything else we could be doing at that time, trusting that the purpose, progress, and even the point is often found in the pause and not always in something we accomplish. Savoring asks us to believe that the present moment is worthy even if we have nothing to show for it—no check marks by the items on our to-do list, no additional money in our bank account, and no emails cleared from our inbox. Savoring understands the moment itself to be the reward.

One realization that will help us practice this discipline is recognizing that this exact moment is fleeting. Understanding that the present moment can only be carried forward as a memory helps us to not take its sacredness for granted. We will live countless meaningful moments throughout our lives. Hopefully we will savor many of them. But none of them will be exactly like this one—the one we are living right this second. Acknowledging this moment as unique will give us the courage to celebrate it.

To begin this celebratory practice of savoring, we must heed the psalmist's words and become people who pay attention to all five of our senses, noticing and naming what we see, hear, taste, smell, and feel.

FROM MY PARENTS' BACK PATIO, I saw the distant lights of boats drifting by in the dark, the laugh lines around my dad's crinkling eyes when he's found something particularly funny, and the dancing flames of candles across the glass table. The evening's soundtrack consisted of rhythmic, lapping waves slapping against the dock, the thud of bean bags hitting the corn hole boards on the lawn, and the distinct sound of my godfather's laugh. The taste of the chocolate chip cookies mixed with espresso lingered in my mouth. The smell of my now-snoozing baby's head resting on my chest mingled with the fresh Seattle scent that was made up of something like lake water and a freshly cut lawn. I felt the weight of Charlie's body, heavy on my chest, and the squeeze of my friend's hand when she listened to me tell her through my tears how grateful I am that God gave me a life I didn't expect or know to pray for.

Notice where you sit right now or choose one scene from a favorite memory. Ask all five of your senses what they remember. Allow them to paint a picture as the setting of your celebration.

Titling the moment and listing all of the feelings associated with the time will help you treasure the experience in the present and in the future when you recall it. Don't put pressure on yourself to make the title particularly creative, just something that cues the joy in your soul when you hear it. "My parents' patio" is enough to transport me back to the deep contentment I felt in my heart that night.

Sometimes we can become overwhelmed by the question "How did you feel?" and are tempted to be too general with our answers and say things like "good" or "not great." As a restoration therapist, I have learned that getting more specific with this question can elicit more poignant responses about how you felt in the moment on which you've chosen to reflect. Instead of asking yourself how you felt, try one of these questions instead:

- How did you feel about yourself in that moment?
- What did that interaction say about the relationship?
- How did you feel about your position in that circumstance?
- What did that exchange communicate to you about your value?
- What message did you hear in the lack of response from your friend?
- How did that action or comment impact your level of emotional safety in that moment?

That night on my parents' patio, I felt treasured, secure, embraced, hopeful, and content. How did you feel about yourself and your situation in the midst of your memory?

Feelings become more powerful when they are not only named but also expressed. Do you welcome the tears that trail down your cheek when a tender feeling touches your heart? Do you laugh with reckless abandon when your joy boils over your inhibitions? Do you clap or jump up and down when your excitement will not be contained? When our eyes notice beauty and our hearts respond with delight and gladness, our bodies want to join the celebration through

144

emotional expression. Laughing, crying, dancing, clapping, skipping, waving—this is embodied joy. This is celebration.

We cement our celebration when we share the details with others. Maybe you've returned home from a vacation and want to describe the place you've traveled to in such detail that it could transport the listener to that destination. Or perhaps you've driven home from the big game and recounted play by play the action that took place on the field and led to the nail-biting victory. Maybe your best friend is getting married, and you sit with her and visualize every detail of her upcoming celebration. Sharing each and every moment heightens the anticipation.

Though some may consider it prideful, research says that acknowledging our victories and gifts can be an important element of savoring—particularly if your experience includes an achievement of a goal or the realization of a hard-won dream. What gifts do you see in yourself through the experience? How did perseverance and discipline take you further than you thought you could go?[2]

I take no credit for the scene that played before me in my parents' backyard—for the husband that calls me his, the little boys that call me "Mama," and the community of family and friends that prayed and praised, grieved and celebrated, alongside me. These are simply gifts.

What I can do—and what I hope you'll do with your own story too—is acknowledge and celebrate the strength that I've gained through my story. My capacity for hope has expanded wider than I knew it could be stretched. I'm making choices to cultivate the courage I need to embrace joy—to not simply touch it but to hold it as something wanted and precious. I am by no means all fixed up and fine. I have not arrived. But today I celebrate that I've grown and I am strong and I am grateful to be a woman who knows hope.

A warning: when it comes to the practice of savoring, we are not fighting on neutral ground. For instance, it's easy for joy in the present moment to be interrupted with thoughts about how the celebration could be better. Suddenly, you have a keen awareness of what *didn't* happen, who *wasn't* there, what *could've* been accomplished, compromising your ability to celebrate what is.

We will dampen our savoring when we choose to reflect on all the reasons that we don't deserve to be honored or to live a life that's worth celebrating. Or maybe you're like me and you struggle to bask in the moment because you feel guilty for celebrating your good gift when so many others don't—a kind of survivor's guilt. When someone congratulates me, the only response I allow myself is, "Thank you! I am so grateful!" This is absolutely true. And it might be a gracious response. But what the other person doesn't know is that while I am deeply grateful, those words are also chosen because I haven't given myself permission to be giddy. How can I celebrate the grace I have been given when I know so many others are still grieving a story that looks different than they had hoped for?

Possibly the most significant barrier to my ability to savor is recalling disappointment in the past and anticipating the same troubles in the future, making it impossible for me to delight in the present. I put an end to any hope before it begins, speaking death over dreams and killing all sense of possibility by focusing on the problems of the past.[3]

Another opposing force as we practice savoring is the hedonic treadmill—a tendency we have as human beings to rapidly adapt to pleasant circumstances or joyful conditions.[4] You have likely experienced this too. You receive good news or an opportunity that you thought would make you want for nothing else, only to find your desire for more growing once again. You've celebrated a goal, only to be haunted by the feeling that it still isn't good enough. The beauty of your view from your front porch has faded into the background of your everyday to where you hardly pause to notice it anymore. But the discipline of savoring will force us to step off this treadmill and appreciate beauty and experience joy as brand-new mercies.

The view from my parents' back patio is the backdrop of thousands of childhood days. But tonight, I see it and celebrate it. I feel content and so deeply connected to the people I love, wrapped in this navy blue fleece blanket with my hair in a messy bun. And I wonder, as we grow in wisdom and live through the years, that if in savoring the small things like a night on the porch with people we love, we will realize that we were actually savoring the big things. Maybe that is the gift of savoring—it reorganizes our priorities and helps us celebrate what matters.

> *Maybe that is the gift of savoring—it reorganizes our priorities and helps us celebrate what matters.*

A CLIENT I SAW OVER the course of several years returned from a lengthy visit to her granddaughter overseas. She had anticipated the trip for months, and when I asked her about it, she paused, seemingly unsure of what to say. Finally, with a dreamy look in her eyes, she said, "I can't tell you one thing that we did—but even now as I reflect on the trip, I see smiles, and I can hear my granddaughter's giggle, and her kiss good-bye still lingers on my cheek."

I smiled, touched by her recollection, and said, "Those sound like the important things."

I'm guessing this was what Jesus was talking about when he gently told Martha that her sister Mary had chosen "what is better" in sitting at His feet (Luke 10:42 NIV). When Jesus and his disciples were traveling, a woman named Martha had kindly opened her home to Him. Understandably, she wanted to provide Him with her best hospitality. The Bible doesn't tell us exactly what her preparations included but we can assume that she wanted to offer a clean home and provide an elaborate meal, perhaps the kind we usually reserve for special occasions. As I might have been, Martha felt overwhelmed and annoyed that her sister Mary was simply sitting at Jesus' feet, soaking in His presence and listening to His wisdom. Jesus gently told Martha that Mary has chosen the better thing by savoring her time with Him and that He will not take that gift from her.

I don't think Jesus was comparing the contemplative life against a life of active service. But I do think He is warning Martha (and you and me) that filling our lives with even the best opportunities and the noblest acts of service come at too great a cost if we are not savoring time with our Savior and one another.

THE COFFEE HAD GONE COLD in the mugs scattered across my parents' patio table, and the large window behind us became a mirror, reflecting the candles as they burned down, one by one. Pockets of people from around the table began to yawn and stand up to leave. Dishes were stacked carefully in the sink. Tupperware was quickly rinsed and returned to its rightful owner. My boys had spent the first portion of their night's sleep on my parents' shoulders and were now being carried up to their beds. Jokes born from wishful thinking were made about our family moving back to the Pacific Northwest someday. I laughed but knew we probably never would. Still, Seattle and the many people we love there will always be with me. They were there to watch me grow. They taught me how to be in so many ways. I watched the last set of taillights climb my parents' steep driveway. I savored the memory of that night, celebrating the small things that, I was learning to see, were actually the big things.

CHAPTER 16

Be Expectant

The only real difference between Anxiety and Excitement
was my willingness to let go of Fear.

Barbara Brown Taylor

DURING THE MAGICAL WEEK BETWEEN Christmas and New Year's Day—
the week often referred to as "no man's land" because no one ever quite
knows what day it is during that week—our family took a trip to the
mountains of Idaho for a week of skiing with my parents and my two
sisters and their husbands. There are few places I feel more at ease than
in this pillowy valley of snow surrounded by the muscled Sawtooth
Mountains. Some places are just special because they hold space for
something that is both rare and necessary. Idaho was a welcome mat
for my dreams, inviting more creative ideas and bolder prayers to take
up residence in my heart. I've often dreamed of making this valley
home. It's wonderful to love where you live. But when your "away"

becomes home, it is, by nature, no longer "away," and I feel protective of the nature of escape in this place.

IT WAS FIVE O'CLOCK IN the morning on New Year's Eve as I sat wide-awake in our dark living room.

It seems to me that there are two ways to celebrate New Year's. One way: sequins, expensive champagne, food you can't pronounce, kisses at midnight, and a bedtime in the early hours of the next year. Another way: pajamas, takeout, games, a mutually agreed upon time to count down to "midnight" with the kids, and going to bed in the same year you woke up.

I fall squarely in the second category. Physically, I like to ease into January and prefer not to take a new year to the face. Also, a fancy New Year's celebration feels like one too many blocks on the tower—like just one more party, one more rich hors d'oeuvre, one more late night just might be the one block that is going to make me topple over. After the festivities of Christmas, I'm ready to simplify and quiet my mind, craving space and serenity over a sparkling spectacle. I've noticed a pattern over a number of years that my anxiety is heightened as we turn the page to a new year. This year, I felt especially anxious and I couldn't sleep.

Admittedly, I struggle with most transitions—a new year, a job change, a new home, the shift from summer's easy cadence to the pressured pace of fall. Objectively, most of the transitions I've experienced are quite positive. But as anyone in my field would probably tell you, pleasant stress (weddings, a new home, becoming a parent) has the same physiological impact on the body as unpleasant stress.

For me, transition is accompanied by a heightened awareness of my dreams and expectations for the chapter ahead. The unknown can be scary, yes, but I am even more terrified that I will be disappointed by my own dreams. I tend to carry audacious ambitions and set lofty goals for myself. And often, the gap between where I am and where I hope I will be leaves me feeling afraid of what might not be.

I've tried being all breezy about the future, minimizing the importance of my dreams to try to make them lighter, but they continue to feel heavy. I've tried to blur the details of the visions I see as I look into the future, but the images remain sharp with clear expectations. You might be the kind of person who is excited and energized by clear vision and big dreams. You maintain an enthusiastic posture, eager for a peek at the goodness that you believe wholeheartedly must be just around the corner. You are not afraid of what you cannot see. You are curious. Expectant. Maybe you are this kind of person. I am not. For me, it feels like being afraid of my own shadow—ever present and terrifying.

I've often gathered in circles with women in prayer where phrases like "Lord, we are expectant" are spoken to God. I have dear friends who share about a new project or season by saying they feel expectant about what is to come. I'm not sure I've ever used this word in a sentence. On the one hand, the word *expectant* sounds slightly demanding and makes God feel a little bit like Santa Claus. When I imagine being expectant, I can't help but picture hands on hips, foot tapping impatiently as I wait to receive exactly what I've asked for.

On the other hand, I am comforted by the safety that must be in the kind of relationship that can hold an expectant heart. A child does not approach a good father with eager expectation without first feeling loved and safe. Perhaps this is the difference between demands and dreams.

LUKE 23 TELLS US ABOUT the character Herod Antipas. He had expectations, not just about who Jesus was but also about what Jesus could do for him. Scripture tells us that when Herod finally met Jesus after a long season of waiting, he was "exceedingly glad" (v. 8 NKJV). Herod had heard many things about Jesus' miracles and he hoped to have Jesus perform a miracle for him. He was more interested in having his wishes granted than he was in a relationship.

Tucked within Herod's expectations of Jesus was a specific vision of what Jesus would be like. He projected his human understanding onto Jesus to fit his own needs. It's easy to excuse ourselves from this mistake. We want to believe that we readily accept the character and will of God instead of handing Him a script for Him to read. We limit God's awesome power and good character to what feels good to us and fits within our own understanding, unable to tolerate mystery or confusion because we need God to work for us in a particular way.

Herod's expectations also carried an agenda. Herod's hope in meeting Jesus was not about encountering and worshipping the Son of God, but about using Him. Herod was intent on a result, not the relationship.

Jesus did not cooperate with Herod's expectations. He did not perform the miracles that Herod demanded of Him that day. And He evaded the questions Herod used to test Him and scrutinize His character. When Jesus refused to be squeezed into a mold made from Herod's personal gain, the chief priests and scribes became angry and vehemently accused Jesus. They could only celebrate Jesus to the degree to which he was willing to meet their own expectations.

In the same way, we are often slow to recognize ourselves standing alongside Herod, the chief priests, and the scribes. I wonder if, like Herod, my own conclusions about the goodness of God are sometimes more invested in the results in my life than in the relationship. I fear my celebration of God and my excitement about His provision hinges on what I think I deserve and might not get. Our expectant hearts become demanding hearts when our delight in Christ is contingent upon God giving power to our own plans. I once heard an idol described as anything in which the outcome has the power to change our view of Christ. As I gaze into the days ahead, full of unknowns and void of guarantees, am I pursuing results that fit my own vision or a relationship with the living God? My fear about the future is an indication of where I currently stand.

As you face your own transitions, what conditions have you placed on God? What are the desires you hold so tightly that their outcomes have the potential to shift your ideas about the goodness of God? How might your relationship with your dreams make you question the character of God if the provision looked different than your vision?

> *Our expectant hearts become demanding hearts when our delight in Christ is contingent upon God giving power to our own plans.*

There is much more imagination in putting our trust in God Himself. Here, our sense of expectancy springs from the assurance of a good and sovereign God. Putting our expectation first doesn't limit the expanse of God's power. But we will merely sip on His faithfulness and take shallow breaths of wonder if our awe of God is limited to the meeting of our own expectations.

Daniel 3 has a prescription for an expectant heart—not a demand rooted in our desires but a belief that blooms from an intimate and right relationship with Christ. King Nebuchadnezzar made an image of gold—an idol. The people were commanded to fall down and worship the image whenever they heard music played by instruments of any kind. At this time, some astrologers came forward and reported to King Nebuchadnezzar that there were some Jews whom the king had set over the affairs of the province of Babylon—Shadrach, Meshach, and Abednego—who were not worshipping the idol that Nebuchadnezzar had instructed.

At hearing this news, the king was furious and summoned the three men. He gave them an ultimatum: either worship the god that he had fashioned or be thrown into the fiery furnace. Shadrach, Meshach, and Abednego replied by telling the king that God will be their defense in this matter, that the true God is able, and they believed He would deliver them from the fiery furnace. And even if He didn't, under no circumstances would they cooperate with his decree (vv. 16–18).

Nebuchadnezzar became angry with their response and ordered the furnace seven times hotter before commanding these men to be bound and thrown into the licking flames. As the king observed his orders being carried out, he shot out of his seat, unable to believe what his eyes were clearly seeing: not three, but four men in the furnace. Nebuchadnezzar recognized the fourth man to be God. When the king ordered the men out, there was no trace of burning anywhere on them.

When faced with a future that was unknown and seemed perilous, Shadrach, Meshach, and Abednego offer examples of what it looks like to have an expectant heart:

- We know that God can.
- We believe that He will.
- And even if He doesn't, we still trust His goodness.

Certainly, Shadrach, Meshach, and Abednego hoped for their preferred outcome. But their celebration of God does not hinge on the conclusion of their story. When threatened, they refused to put God's character on trial. Shadrach, Meshach, and Abednego were filled with expectation and void of presumption.

Regardless of the outcome, we will celebrate that God will be who He says He is. Can we empty ourselves of demands to be filled with delight in God in the same way? As we look at the season ahead, will we allow our awe of God to expand beyond the limits of our own imagination?

FOSTERING AN EXPECTANT HEART FOR the future requires committing to gratitude in the present—the ability to notice and appreciate who God is in the midst of what your life looks like right now. Unedited. No additions. No subtractions. Many of us have been told a story that celebration can only follow good news and that a change in circumstances or a shift in a relationship is required before we can experience joy.

But the secret to cultivating joy in the future is to celebrate the life we are living now. Not only does gratitude expand our ability to experience joy in the here and now, it also allows us to see possibilities instead of the problems we fear—even if those problems have plagued our past.

The secret to cultivating joy in the future is to celebrate the life we are living now.

Imagine opening the door on tomorrow or the season ahead. Do you let the door creak open with caution, wondering if God is who He says He is based on whether or not He will meet your expectations, hoping He will but fearing He won't? Or, do you throw open the door with an expectant heart, excited about what God could do with your life and what purpose He has planned for you in the coming days? With God's steadfast character as a constant we can count on, an expectant heart revives our imagination and broadens our vision for the future. Gratitude gives us the freedom to dream.

Maybe you're emerging from a season of waiting and longing. Or perhaps the last season has mostly been characterized by disappointment and loss. Possibly, you've found redemption in the wake of what felt wrecked and ruined. Yet, it still feels like your joy is locked somewhere inside a different set of circumstances.

One fact that gives me hope is that we have more power over our sense of joy than we typically believe. Joy will not simply come with a transition; joy comes with a transformation of the heart. We are not able to control our circumstances, but we can make choices about what we look for and, therefore, find. We can make decisions about when and how we connect with other people in our community. And we are empowered to decide whether or not we will allow our circumstances to be an avenue of growth in our lives.

Our imagination, like most gifts, can be used destructively or constructively. It can be a weapon wielded to escape reality, to numb the hurt we've experienced, or to anesthetize the pain of a future we fear. But our imagination can also be where we go to encounter reality, to run into the truth of a steadfast God who holds our dreams in His good and sovereign hands.

On the precipice of a new chapter, my expectant heart offers me little certainty. My hard work will not yield any guarantees. I know exactly one thing about the year ahead, and this one's for both of us: God is who He says He is and He will do immeasurably more than we can ask or imagine. The great exchange He made on the cross—our sin for His righteousness—is proof He already has.

Joy will not simply come with a transition; joy comes with a transformation of the heart.

I stood up to make the morning's pot of coffee. Soon, this room would be a flurry of winter clothing: down jackets draped over chairs, people shuffling around with one ski sock in hand in search of its match, and mittens stuffed with hand warmers for the cold morning. Before the gleeful chaos ensued, I opened the door to feel the shocking chill of Idaho's winter air, glimpsing at the cobalt Idaho sky. I squared my shoulders toward the mountains and toward my waiting future. There are no guarantees there, but there is promise. I will not fear its pain or its plenty.

CHAPTER 17

Share the Good News

"…and really, it wasn't much good having anything exciting
like floods, if you couldn't share them with somebody."

A.A. Milne, *Winnie-the-Pooh*

THE SCENE INSIDE MY HOUSE felt like the eye of a hurricane. Like a puppy
scratching at the door, James was eager to play outside. As is the case
most years in early April, the weather over the past several weeks had
been more favorable for "house cats" than "puppy dogs" like James.
Today was a continuation of the same—a sharp wind blew through
the thinly leafed trees and the sky was brushed with the colors of a
Renoir painting—dark and moody.

Charlie, nearly thirteen months old, was squealing in delight in
reaction to his brother's entertainment. Someone's enthusiastic arm
had knocked over a half-eaten cereal bowl and a slow trickle of milk
was now cascading off the countertop like a late summer's waterfall.

The fact that I even heard the delivery person's knock on our door was a miracle. I wasn't expecting a package and was intrigued as I brought it inside. Seeing the return address was from Georgia was the sunshine the day needed.

I quickly opened it as I spoon-fed Charlie the last of his snack and instructed James to leave the large yard toys outside. I carefully pulled sheets of tissue tucked around a beautiful, handmade blanket, knitted in the sweetest soft gray. This friend knew of my love for neutrals.

As I absentmindedly rubbed my swollen belly, I realized just how much I needed someone to share our good news with us. Though I had safely given birth to two beautiful boys, pregnancy remained a risk for me and we had a few scares that had threatened her life already. My rising hormone levels were an indication the pregnancy was healthy and progressing as it should, but they were accompanied by vicious and persistent migraine headaches that made it difficult to manage everyday tasks. Still, every ache and pain was a sign that our little girl was thriving. Though we knew we wanted more children, her story was different than the boys'. She came to us somewhat unexpectedly and quickly after Charlie. I was sure the news of a third baby was too good to be true and a part of me felt embarrassed by the riches. We knew that if we were blessed to meet her, we would call her Annie Michelle—my two sisters' middle names that combined happen to mean "a gift of grace from God," which of course is just exactly what she is. Our good news of Annie is a testimony of God's kindness to us, and it increased my joy to share that good news of the abundant nature of His love with a friend.

THE APOSTLE PAUL USED THE Greek word *chara*, which means "joy," in three different ways in Scripture. He refered to it as a gift of the Holy Spirit when he listed the fruits of the Spirit in his letter to the Galatians (Gal 5:22). He spoke of this kind of joy often as a result of suffering for Christ's sake (Col 1:24, 2 Cor 6:10, I Peter 4:13, Heb 10:34)—a

SHARE THE GOOD NEWS

kind of joy I had spent years befriending in the midst of my own story of struggle and loss. But Paul also used *chara* to refer to the progress in the faith of believers (1 Thes 2:19, Phil 2:2)—a result of sharing the Good News and the gift of sometimes catching a glimpse of how this news is transforming people's lives.[1]

Upon reflection, this made sense to me. I come from a family who loves to share good news. We even call my youngest sister "the town crier." She can keep a secret if she must but she loves to deliver information and be the bearer of good news. I knew the joy it brought me to sit in front of a client who had endured a season of struggle and tell them that I had hope for them and their future, even if they couldn't yet see it for themselves. I felt delight in telling James that there were only five days left until Christmas and in saying, "Surprise!" to my mom when we flew across the country to surprise her on her birthday.

Modern psychology has a term for this: Capitalization. Many studies confirm that not only does our overall well-being benefit from sharing vulnerably with others about our struggles and accessing the support of our community, but also in sharing good news with others. Delivering good news and celebrating its effects with others increases our joy.

This was the very reason that joy marked the early life of the church. Acts 13 tells the story of missionaries Paul and Barnabas traveling to Antioch in Pisidia, where Paul gave his first recorded sermon. In his speech, he reviewed the history of God's people and reiterated God's promises to them. He encouraged the audience by telling them that they were recipients of the fulfillment of these promises through Jesus! The good news is not just for other people but also for them!

The people must have been excited because the news spread, and the following week a larger crowd gathered to hear Paul speak (v. 44). However, some of the Jews became jealous of Paul and Barnabas' popularity. Because they felt threatened, they went to the most respected men and women of the city and convinced them that they would lose their lifestyles as they knew them if they listened to this teaching, and as a result, Paul and Barnabas were driven out of the city (v. 50). But scripture tells us that in spite of their hardships, of which they would suffer many, they were filled with the joy of the Holy Spirit.

As news of the gospel spread, joy increased. What this means for you and me is that telling others about the ultimate joy available to us through Jesus will always delight us and give us something to celebrate. Whether we are sharing the good news of the gospel with someone who does not yet know the hope of Jesus or sharing the good news of how He is transforming our hearts, a relationship, or making a way for joy in circumstances that seemed hopeless, spreading the good news of Christ's movement in our lives will increase our joy.

Sometimes we hesitate to share good news because we are afraid our celebration will cause others sorrow. We've connected deeply with others in our shared experience. So when we encounter celebration, we fear our joy will mean abandoning others who we love but no longer share our circumstances. We measure our pain against others' hurt and grow quiet and even feel guilty when we perceive our pain as "less." We feel dissonance in our differences. Yet, I've learned that both sorrow and celebration are best practiced not through the denial of the other, but with the keen awareness that both exist at all times and that God is present and working in both places. Pain and joy do not cancel each other out. They are tender companions. It is better to hold one another where we are than to hide our realities from one another.

Often, many of us feel timid in sharing the gospel with others or telling people what a difference knowing Jesus has made in our lives. One truth that gives me courage is that as we see in the example of Paul and Barnabas, this joy is promised to us regardless of the outcome. Our excitement in sharing about Jesus will not be contingent upon others' reactions—their acceptance or lack of acceptance of us or who Christ is or what He has done for them. What makes this celebration unique to other joys we experience on earth is that this joy is a gift of the Holy Spirit and is, therefore, not circumstantial (Galatians 5:22). The joy of the Holy Spirit is not a gift that comes only after a victory or a yes. To those who have put their trust in Jesus, this gift is available to us now. Joy is not a feeling but a fact for those who receive Christ—our inheritance as His children.

When you begin to tell others about who Jesus is and the difference He has made in your own life, you will see that joy is cyclical in nature. Our hearts may be burdened with struggles like disappointment, loss, or loneliness. But as followers of Christ, we have access to a delight that is not extinguished by these experiences. And as we celebrate this thrill, the joy of the Lord draws others to Jesus, who is of course, the source of all joy. And as we share the good news with others, it increases our own sense of gladness.

As I was folding the blanket back up, a letter fell out. It was addressed to Annie Michelle—my unborn baby girl.

> Here is a special blanket, made just for you, and there's quite a story behind it! One day, when you're older, you can ask your mom to tell you about it. It's a story about you, your mom and dad . . . but most of all, it's a story about the tender mercy of a loving God!
>
> I have loved every minute of making this blanket for you! Every stitch, knot and turn, have been reminders of God's tender mercy . . . You will notice at least one imperfection: a black spot where it seems there was a problem with the color/dye. I thought about cutting the yarn at that point and rejoining it again, to "hide" the imperfection. But then I realized that the "imperfection" was there for a reason as a reminder of God's grace and unconditional love and acceptance, a reminder that our value does not depend on our performance or the idea of being perfect.
>
> The truth is that most of us try hard to "hide" our imperfections,

our struggles, our fear, our vulnerability, the dark "spots" in our story, including our pain, suffering, sorrow, and loss. Something singular about my relationship with your mom is that I've never felt I had to "hide" my dark spots from her. She is a safe person who understands the trap of perfectionism and performance (the fear of failure and making mistakes), and how these are clues to deeper matters-of-the-heart: messages about love and trust, identity and safety, belonging and agency. In time you will understand more about the significance of the "dark" spot . . . it is there for a reason.

I want you to know that making this blanket for you has given me great comfort and joy. I hope that, in some small way, this blanket will bring a measure of comfort and joy to you as well!

The sweet gray baby blanket is a beloved gift I will always cherish and knowing the meaning behind each stitch—especially the "imperfect" one—makes it priceless. The blanket reminded me of the Navajo weavers who intentionally weave a flaw into their work, to remind them that only God is perfect.[2] In sharing with my friend the good news of our little girl, my friend was reminding me of the best news that is true for all of us—that Christ's strength is made perfect in our weakness (2 Corinthians 12:9).

JOHN 15 TELLS US THAT there is great joy in this truth. Jesus used an allegory of a vine with branches to impress upon His disciples—and us—the life-giving hope of remaining in His love. The main purpose of using this particular allegory is to emphasize the disciples' dependence on Him—and in doing so, they flourish! Jesus continued by saying that He had loved His disciples in the way that His Father had loved Him. Also, when the disciples kept Jesus' commands, they would remain "intimately at home in His love," just as He had made a home in His Father's love by keeping His commands (vv. 15:9–10

THE MESSAGE). Finally, Jesus said that His purpose in sharing this with the disciples was so that His joy can be their joy, and their joy would be complete (v. 11).

Our joy is made complete when we know that our weakness is an invitation to depend on Christ. Each time I wrap my daughter in this handmade blanket, I will give thanks for the good news of her life. And every time my eyes take notice of the imperfect stitch, I will remember the good news of the joy that comes from remaining in Christ's love. And I will pray that this joy becomes my little girl's joy too.

CHAPTER 18

Learn to Play

Joy does not simply happen to us. We have to choose joy
and keep choosing it every day.

Henri J.M. Nouwen

THIS IS WHAT I SEE: Celebration is more active than passive—more of
a choice than an outcome. Certainly we can be surprised by joy. But
finding joy is more of a hunt than a stroll. And this hunt becomes
more essential when joy feels scarce, beauty seems rare, and there is
no obvious cause for celebration. Like most good things in life, this
search is both challenging and essential, especially now.

THE WORLD HAS BEEN SIDESWIPED by a global pandemic, causing
disruption and, for some, devastation. Jobs have been impacted, health
and safety cannot be taken for granted, cancellations have wiped
calendars clean of commitments, and mental health struggles have

become more acute. Our small town is beginning to buckle under the virus's impact. Local shops' window displays have been substituted for For Lease signs. The stores will probably be replaced by something depressing like a CVS drugstore or a Chase Bank. The sidewalks are mostly empty. Parks are roped off. Connection is scarce. Relationships are starving.

It's been a unique season in my career as a therapist. Of course there are always themes that emerge in the human experience, but never has my entire caseload of clients been struggling through the same collective circumstance. By my observation, as a group, we have generally moved through irritation, depressed moods and hopelessness, fear of the unknown, acceptance and resilience, and growth with varying degrees of success. Included in the growth part, I think, is this hunt for joy.

That's what my boys and I are doing today. We are searching, stepping over kelp that looks like large chocolate-brown lasagna noodles, trudging up and down our local beach, which is a bit of a mixed dish: sand, rocks, broken shells, just a little bit of trash, and sea glass. In the last few months, with few other activities available to us, we have been on nearly every beach on the Connecticut and Rhode Island coastline, hunting for sea glass—our eyes trained for shades of Kelly green, amber, cobalt and aqua blues, and frosted white. We live in a town with two colleges nearby so sea glass of the brown variety is particularly plentiful. Also, the line between sea glass and glass by the sea becomes blurred. On Sunday mornings, many of these pieces of "sea glass" look as if they could spend a few more nights being churned by the salt and sand. Sometimes we keep the questionable pieces and sometimes we toss them back in to let the wind and waves have their way with the sharp edges. It's not lost on me that this is also what is happening to us.

Charlie is strapped to my front, stuffed in a BabyBjörn in his snowsuit that keeps him both warm and immobile. I look like I'm wearing a giant navy blue, five-pointed star on my ever-growing belly and my hair is wind-wild as I drink irresponsible amounts of coffee from my thermos. James has no direct route or apparent strategy in his search and looks much like the sandpiper birds frenetically scurrying about on the beach. God gave James a double measure of joy and every piece of sea glass he finds is met with the same level of enthusiasm as if it's his first. Occasionally, he bends low over the rocks, sorting his treasure as if he's counting the beads of an abacus. Some pieces are obvious as if placed as a gift by fellow sea-glass sojourners. Other pieces lay stealthily under shallow, languid waters.

Both my four-year-old son and my four-year-old self love to hunt for sea glass. I am, and have always been, a collector by nature. I love to watch a collection grow, but more than half the fun of collecting is not the accumulated items themselves but the hunt. I've learned from the collector in me that the more we search, the more we see. Like when you're considering purchasing a particular car and suddenly it seems like everyone has had the same idea and you spot it everywhere on the highway. The more we seek beauty, pursue joy, and count the reasons to celebrate, the more beauty we will find. And this joy is not insignificant or frivolous. When we choose to delight in the faces of the people we love or in the colors of the flowers that stab through the thawing earth and bloom in rebellious celebration, we become active participants of hope—characters in a story that insist that what is most obvious is not all there is.

Sometimes we live our stories waiting for God to inject us with His joy. Certainly, He can and does do this. But often, joy is experienced to the degree we are willing to contribute and partake—participating in Christ's hope regardless of whether or not we have an obvious reason to do so. This requires being obedient to God, trusting truth over the very real feelings we might be experiencing in that moment. It means seeing that the kingdom of God is here and is now, instead of a destination on the horizon. And it looks like naming and marking the many ways in which God has shown His power and kindness to us.

It's easy to think that celebration should come easily. It's understandable that if, like me, you're a little irritated that even the delightful gift of celebration requires effort and intention at times.

It is, admittedly, both difficult and freeing for me to consider celebration as a discipline. It's difficult because it feels like celebration should be a reflex, not something that requires practice. When we are invited to speak truth or celebrate in the midst of challenging circumstances, the statement I hear most often from my counseling clients and from the voice inside my own head is "But I don't feel it." I understand the desire to feel celebratory before we act celebratory. But what I have learned the hard way is that most often the feelings we love to feel follow actions. As my friend and colleague, Wib, says, "We can think and act our way to a new feeling. We cannot feel our way to a new way of thinking and acting." In other words, if we want to feel something different, we usually have to do something different.

But it's also freeing to recognize celebration as a discipline because through this lens, celebration is available to me and to you at all times.

THE BOOK OF ECCLESIASTES INSISTS on this truth and invites us to practice a life of joy. Ecclesiastes 11:7–10 describes this life of joy, telling us that enjoyment is to be lifelong—not limited to a given season or reserved only for the young. God's radical celebration is not a feast set aside for some but for all. There is no prerequisite. You don't have to be accomplished or fit into that fancy dress you haven't worn in fifteen years or be married, recently promoted, or have perfectly behaved children. Celebration is for you. And celebration is for today, in this moment, not only for the dream down the road or back in the "good old days."

This passage is also careful to point out that joy is both an internal experience and an external expression. In other words, the condition of our hearts and the way that we see are twin pillars of joy. The discipline to celebrate is both an inside job and an outside job. It includes a commitment to address the lies we tell ourselves with truth about why we matter and what will actually make us feel secure. It requires dedication to focus our attention on what is good and practice rejoicing right here, right now.

The rhythm of our daily walks on the beach, hunting for colors in the sand, is our family's stake in the ground that we are here to notice and celebrate beauty and experience joy in this season. Celebration is our protest. What began as a means of entertaining my boys during months characterized by cancellations and closures has become our everyday practice of noticing, appreciating, and savoring the goodness—our practice of celebration.

THERE IS A DISTINCT AND crucial difference between celebration and escape. Celebration is able to hold the reality of pain and joy at the same time. It acknowledges and grieves the many evidences that our world is not how it should be. But it is also firm in its conviction that the kingdom of God is coming and is also here right now.

Celebration is able to hold the reality of pain and joy at the same time.

I was talking with a client recently whose mom is suffering with a terminal illness. She told me about playing cards with her mom and laughing so hard during the conversation that her iced tea came out of her nose. "Am I still being honest about my grief if I was able to laugh with my mom in the midst of it?" she asked.

Celebration is not a means of escaping the reality that our hearts are brutally bruised but keeps us grounded in the truth that both our heartache and our hope are true. That's one of the things I love about the gospel: the cross makes it clear that both are real. The discipline of delight is not pretending. Celebration is not avoidance.

Escape, on the other hand, keeps us numb and tells us that our only hope in coping with the brokenness we see and feel is to leave. Of course leaving doesn't always look like physically standing up and walking out. We check out mentally by disengaging from conversations that threaten our ideas about how the world should work. We numb our emotions instead of addressing them, deciding that healing is too much work and too painful to pursue. We can numb in all manner of ways. We find it easier to entertain ourselves with other people's problems on the television screen than acknowledging our own. We shop and accumulate, gathering without ever feeling like we have enough. We eat, stuffing ourselves but never feeling fulfilled. We drink and take drugs to anesthetize the hurt, only to experience more pain when the effects wear off.

Another key difference is that celebration is an empowered action and escape is a coping reaction. Celebration looks at a broken world and recognizes that while we are not in total control, there are actions we can take and choices we can make to acknowledge God's goodness, practice celebration, and participate in hope. Escape looks at a broken world and decides there is absolutely nothing we can do to make our feelings or circumstances different and settles for temporary pleasure. These fleeting indulgences solve nothing and leave us with the very pain we were trying desperately to avoid in the first place.

Ecclesiastes 2:1–11 is also careful to point out the difference between joy and pleasure-seeking and to expose the failure of the latter. The author describes in detail the many ways in which he never denied himself or refused his heart any pleasure (v. 10 NIV) and concluded that everything was meaningless and nothing was gained (v. 11 NIV). Pleasure-seeking is an imitation of joy—a mere illusion.

Celebration is God's healing balm for our broken world and to our scarred hearts. It is the exercise of actively remembering and enjoying the goodness of God in our lives.

Perhaps you have seen joy and discipline as somewhat mutually exclusive or opposing forces. At the very least, maybe you have perceived joy coming as a reward for an accomplishment achieved through discipline. But joy is not the opposite of discipline; it is the key to discipline. According to Nehemiah, it is the very thing that makes us strong. As he said, "The joy of the LORD is your strength" (Nehemiah 8:10 NIV). This joy propels us to practice celebration even when it appears we haven't been given a reason to do so.

Celebration is God's healing balm for our broken world and to our scarred hearts.

We recently washed and sorted all of our pieces of sea glass by color, laying long strips of paper towels across our kitchen table and countertops. We've considered projects including mosaics and filling glass lamps with our collection. Friends and family members have offered their ideas as they've watched our collection grow. But for now at least, a simple oversized glass jar to contain every piece feels like the most appropriate way to celebrate the season—a capsule to remind us to hunt for beauty, collect goodness, and to celebrate the joy we find.

This hunt for joy has become less of a pastime and more of a necessity for me. My own private pain ran parallel to the collective struggle of the pandemic. As the girl who prides herself on being able to do hard things, I'm not inclined to acknowledge those difficulties as a threat. But a conversation with my mentor, Terry, forced my battle into the open and placed it squarely at the center of my focus.

"I THINK I'M BURNED-OUT," I told Terry who was framed by the twelve-inch screen of my computer. I was met with comforting eyes and silence that invited me to continue. "I've lost my sense of taste. Not for food per se, although we could argue that is the case too. But also for fun, for humor, for spontaneity, for beauty." I was sure that on most days, I blew past most of those delights, failing to notice them entirely. But when I did catch sight of signs of life in the light, I also struggled to absorb them.

"Migraines join me on more days than not," I continued. "A couple of months ago, my hormones took a running start before diving off a cliff. The muscles in my shoulders feel more like stone than tissue. And while we're on the subject of my shoulders, they appear to rest a few inches higher than they should. As if they're caught on something." As a staunch overcomer, I viewed these physical symptoms as something to conquer, rather than signs to yield to.

Terry listened intently before saying with both compassion and practicality, "I think you are burnt-out." He didn't end with this confirmation. "And, if you don't start listening and heeding these signs that you've identified, you'll likely have the privilege of walking through depression."

I can't recall whether my response was a thought or an inaudible whisper: "I think I already am."

Depending on who you are or with whom you talk to, I may or may not have fit into the neat box of major depressive disorder drawn by the DSM-5, the *Diagnostic and Statistical Manual of Mental Disorders*. The root system of depression is intricate and it has many branches. But that's not the point. The point was that with or without a diagnosis, my body was telling me that there was something very wrong.

Obviously righting this ship would require unhurried time, putting names to feelings that were driving this behavior, shedding layers of faulty thinking, and many intentional changes, including returning to work with my own therapist for a season. But Terry suggested that a good starting place would be to do something fun (in which the only goal was fun) at least twice a week.

"What do you do for fun?" he asked.

I felt embarrassed that even after a few seconds past an awkward pause, I could not name one thing. There were many things I enjoyed about my life and found meaningful and connecting. But nothing that came to mind fit neatly into the category of fun without also bleeding into a project, obligation, or goal.

I thought my prolonged silence would release me from having to come up with an immediate answer, but Terry was undeterred.

Finally I said, "I like to explore. I like to take my boys to New York City and get ice cream at Van Leeuwen's—a local ice cream shop with delicious vegan options. I like to take them to Central Park to run in Sheep Meadow or find a new playground to explore while we wait for Jimmy to finish work a couple of blocks away."

Terry's silent nod bid me to continue.

"And when I'm by myself in New York City, I like to overpay for an almond milk latte from a local coffee shop and explore an independent bookstore without interruption. I enjoy wandering the streets of the quieter neighborhoods in the city like Greenwich Village and admiring the architecture of the brownstones, exploring new shops and making note of restaurants I'd like to return to with Jimmy. I also love to go to Broadway shows but can't afford to do that often."

Once I began to name the fun, it was like an avalanche—one thought collected another and then another.

"I also like to sit with a friend—usually just one, but maybe two—and have a meaningful conversation without a care about the time. Because it's not quite the same when it's a coffee date that's shoved into a gap in my therapy client schedule or squeezed in before a school pick-up or an errand. Really good conversations need room to breathe and are best served when people can come before projects."

Terry nodded before saying, "Those activities are just as important as anything else you do during the week. Do them."

So I began the slow progress of programming my brain to see the purpose in fun. I felt a kindred spirit in the author of Ecclesiastes, who questioned the function and meaning of fun: "'Laughter,' I said, 'is madness. And what does pleasure accomplish?'" (Ecclesiastes 2:2 NIV).

But just as God is the author of wisdom, He is the inventor of fun.

But just as God is the author of wisdom, He is the inventor of fun. We need not look beyond His creation to spot God's humor and sense of adventure in the midst of the created order. A giraffe cleans its ear with its twenty-one inch tongue! The effort it takes for an adult female flamingo to raise her young drains her of her bright pink hue.[1]

LIKE ME, ULTIMATELY THE AUTHOR of Ecclesiastes puts his weight on the truth that fun is not frivolous but a homemade gift from God, crafted with intention. He's encouraged by the notion that "God takes pleasure in *your* pleasure!" (Ecclesiastes 9:7 THE MESSAGE). Used properly, fun is not a cheap escape from our reality but an avenue rich with invitations to connect with God and the people He has placed beside us.

Like sea glass, taking care to seek these opportunities for fun and actually picking them up requires not only spotting them but also seeing the value in each one. Because some of these shining moments of hope, these flashes of delight, and gracious gifts will be visible and some will be almost hidden, but none of them will force their way into your pocket. None of them will collect unless you choose to gather them. And both the collecting and the treasures themselves just might be the grace you need.

My own jar of treasures in this season looks something like this: the curve of baby Charlie's cheek, the comfort of Jimmy's favorite T-shirt that I have now claimed as my own, the blushing morning sky, witnessing a counseling client's transformation, friends that surprised me by singing "Happy Birthday" in my front yard.

Even the mundane and seemingly unpleasant elements of motherhood—dry Play-Doh smashed in the cracks of floorboards, the whir of the sound machine, and crusted spit-up running down the sleeves of most of my shirts—are markers that God has moved in my story. Treasures. Your jar might be made up of different collections, some easy to spot and celebrate and some less obvious but signs of God's faithfulness nonetheless.

This hunt for sea glass—and for goodness—is a tradition we are committed to carrying forward as a family. When I hold the pieces that have been worn by the salt and sand, their edges rounded and their texture smooth, I wonder if this is exactly what God is doing for us—smoothing out our sharp edges. Sea glass tells the story of the cross. Jesus, broken and crushed, became our greatest treasure. It's a tangible reminder of what God's love has been doing all along: making us into something new.

Maybe our reasons to celebrate have changed but they are not gone. They are bent toward the enduring aspects of this life. Will we let these challenging seasons—the seasons we would write differently—make us into something new? We have a choice. Will we move our bodies toward beauty, physically touching it, putting one foot in front of the other to look for it? Will we let the salt heal our wounds? How will our family and friends remember us when they reflect on this time? Will we be active and not passive in our hunt for joy? Will we step beyond noticing beauty to actually celebrate what we see? Will we find the courage to celebrate the fact that the truths that matter are still true?

CHAPTER 19

Rhythms and Rituals

I cannot transform myself, or anyone else for that matter. What I can do is create the conditions in which spiritual transformation can take place, by developing and maintaining a rhythm of spiritual practices that keep me open and available to God.

Ruth Haley Barton

THE TRAFFIC ON THE HUTCHINSON River Parkway, or "the Hutch" as most of us locals call it, was particularly congested as James, Charlie, and I made our way to the Upper West Side neighborhood of Manhattan on a Friday afternoon in late June. Jimmy's office is at Lincoln Center—one block off Central Park—and the boys and I had a tradition of driving into Manhattan to play in the city for a few hours every Friday afternoon and picking Jimmy up at his office for an early dinner before heading home after rush hour.

The activities varied. On rainy days, we often visited the giant dinosaur exhibit at the Museum of Natural History and afterward, Shake Shack across the street for burgers, fries, and milkshakes. On warmer days, we often frequented one of our favorite playgrounds in Central Park, Manhattan's skyline peeking over the leafy horizon of the iconic park. Sometimes we just aimlessly wandered around the winding paths. The boys would sprint and toddle under bridges and across lawns, stopping frequently to stare at street performers or to watch a horse and buggy clip-clop down the street.

Sometimes we meet Jimmy at his office, which makes me feel like I'm the ringmaster of an unruly circus blowing through the quiet offices. On most Fridays, Jimmy meets us in the park for a picnic dinner before we make one last stop for ice cream at Van Leeuwen's. It hardly feels like a trip to the city without ice cream from Van Leeuwen's.

When I was pregnant with James, I gave Jimmy a children's book for Christmas called *Every Friday*. It is a sweet book with darling illustrations that tells the story of a father and son who shared a tradition of spending time together each Friday morning, visiting the same places and enjoying the same food together each week. Manhattan on a Friday afternoon was our *"Every Friday"*—our weekly celebration.

One of the things I love most about living in Connecticut is that we are just about an hour outside of New York City. In our early days of living on the East Coast, I felt energized by the city but it also represented loss because it was so "other" to the life I loved on the West Coast and had left behind. It was a place that consistently reminded me that I was not at home. But over the years, it has become a place of delight—a place for memory making, connection, and creativity. It's played host to moments of profound growth and celebration for both Jimmy and me, and now, our kids.

Living in a quiet, quaint coastal town suits us, with our pajamas, flip-flops, and coffee in hand. We are s'mores-in-the-front-yard-firepit and sea-glass-hunting-at-the-beach people. But on Fridays, I love being a city person. I know I can't just pop in on a Friday afternoon for an ice cream cone and jaunt in the park and call myself a "city person," and I make no claim that I am a true New Yorker. But I do love the city and I'll always be grateful for its essential role in helping me adjust, accept, and, eventually, fall in love with the East Coast.

Rituals and traditions serve as signposts, signaling our senses to celebrate. Whether it's a traditional meal, wearing a particular attire, or gathering together in the same place at a certain time of the week, our senses record the sights, smells, tastes, sounds, and feel of these traditions and they become the ushers that guide us to our place in a different kind of mental, emotional, spiritual, or physical space.

A friend of mine used to reminisce about how her mom would open the windows and play classical music as the sun set on Saturday while the smell of homemade cinnamon raisin bread wafted through the house, signaling the beginning of family Sabbath. Whenever she recalled this memory, her shoulders would instantly relax and she'd put away her work almost without thinking. She also insisted that her family's traditions and rituals around Sabbath significantly deepened her family members' relationships and cemented her faith as she transitioned into adulthood.

Years ago, I saw a teenage boy in my counseling practice who was polite and kind but a young man of few words. I struggled to know how to connect with him. But after a few weeks I noticed that he brought a cold can of Coca-Cola to every single session. I didn't mention it to him, but I made a mental note of it. The next week when he walked into my office, I handed him a cold can of Coca-Cola and said, "These are on me from now on." The smile he offered me in return will remain one of the highlights of my career. This attention to detail and small ritual shifted something in him and became his cue to settle more securely into our conversations.

Rituals are rhythms and celebrations that invite us to new emotional places and spiritual spaces.

For me, the first glimpse of the George Washington Bridge as I cruise down the West Side Highway along the Hudson River is the view that tells me it's time to play. A mere glance at the bridge is enough to help me lean in toward acceptance and gratitude—to appreciate the week for exactly what it had to offer—even if it didn't match my expectations. This is my invitation to take an expansive breath, extending my capacity for joy and to dig deep in my hunt for delight.

Rituals are rhythms and celebrations that invite us to new emotional places and spiritual spaces.

Today in Central Park, I'm sipping an iced coffee with extra almond milk as I push Charlie in a baby swing with one hand, keeping one eye on James as he struggles to manage the monkey bars. I can see his knuckles turning white from where I stand, his lanky body dangling, belly button and underwear peeking out from his blue jeans.

"You have to let go in order to grasp the next bar, honey!" I yell across the playground. Naturally, this requires more courage and strength than his four-year-old self has. James' clammy hands slip off the metal bar trying to reach the next one before falling a short distance to the ground. And then he tries again, undeterred. I breathe deeply, listening to Charlie babble and the sound of taxis honking like a flock of geese in the distance. I can smell the blooming spring flowers and the ever-so-faint odor of horse manure from the overpriced carriage rides that cater to tourists. The warmth of the sun feels more intense on my face than it has in months, likely expanding the multi-lane highway that is beginning to form on the surface of my forehead. My shoulders are more relaxed. My priorities feel like they are listed in the right order: the things I say matter most to me actually do in this moment. God's voice is tender and His truth is a little bit easier to believe. On the playground, His presence is subtle, but I sense it.

EVER SINCE THE ISRAELITES EXPERIENCED what we now refer to as Passover and left Egypt, God has instituted rituals and traditions in the form of sacrifices, feasts, and rhythms as a means of bringing us into His holy presence. These rituals were never designed to be the hope that saves us but rather the celebration that shepherds us toward the hope of Christ. In Numbers 10, God gave instructions to His people regarding two silver trumpets—how they are to be used, who should sound the trumpets, what it means when only one instrument is blown, and what it means when two instruments are blown. My favorite instruction is naturally God's command surrounding celebration where He told His people to blow the trumpets on their days of rejoicing over feasts and offering and sacrifices so that their attention would remain on God and they would remember Him and what He has done (v. 10). In fact, a common characteristic of those early celebrations was that they were often noisy and tumultuous. Since the early days of God's people, the sights, sounds, smells, tastes, and touches of each tradition are our attendants, walking us back to belonging, where we are both secure and free.

God's people are marked by celebration—they are known for it. It is an essential part of their identity as God's people. It strikes me that one becomes known for something not by telling other people that it is important and matters to them but by practicing it. I spent years telling myself and other people that celebration was a valuable part of the Christian faith and that it mattered to me. I sat in my leather chair across from countless clients on my couch, helping them find the courage to rest—to remember that they are not merely instruments to use but God's image bearers—His prized kid, and that they are just as cherished in the pause as they are in the push.

I have nodded my head in conversations with friends as we discussed that delighting in God and the many ways He reaches us with His world is time well spent. I'm not yet sure if I am a person who is marked by celebration. It takes commitment and practice over the course of time for a trait to become a virtue. But I am becoming a person who is intentional about practicing celebration. And I will call myself a celebrator. Because even as I practice, fail, and try again, God has already knit celebration into my identity as His child made in His image.

To profess that we value celebration and to practice it in a way in which it becomes a defining characteristic of who we are requires that we celebrate beyond when it is convenient.

The Bible discusses several feasts and festivals celebrated by God's people. Passover was celebrated to remember their deliverance from Egypt. The Feast of Firstfruits was a feast in which they expressed gratitude for the harvest and acknowledged their dependence on God. The Feast of Booths celebrated God's protection of His people during the years they wandered in the desert. The Feast of Weeks—also known as Pentecost—celebrated the end of the wheat harvest. This was the one festival in which leavened bread was a part of the celebration, representing and foreshadowing the day when gentiles (non-Jews) would be brought into the family of God. Rosh Hashanah, also known as the Feast of Trumpets, is the Jewish New Year. The ten days between Rosh Hashanah and the Day of Atonement, when the priest could enter the temple and atone for people's sins the previous year, is often referred to as the "days of awe" where the people delighted in God in a way that produced righteousness. The Day of Atonement is considered a feast, but the people fasted on this day, celebrating God's abundant provision.

Each of these celebrations occurred not because the people felt that they had earned the feast or because they were in the mood to celebrate but because it was time to do so. Even Sabbath didn't come as a reward for the week's accomplishments. A day of rest wasn't simply the result of exhaustion from the past week. It was, and continues to be, a structure of celebration that invites us to release our grip on control and step into God's rhythms of grace. Celebration starts when it starts.

What this means for you and me is that we can't afford to wait until life feels calm, but should instead celebrate in the center of chaos. We don't have to wait until we feel we have a suitable reason to celebrate. We can celebrate that the person and presence of Jesus gives us a permanent reason to rejoice. Rituals and traditions such as the Sabbath are the structure that allows us to celebrate regardless of our personal circumstances. They are a response to God's command to remember Him—who He is and what He has done to set us free. In Deuteronomy 6,

Celebration doesn't start when we feel we've earned it, it starts when it starts.

God gave the Israelites instructions on how to love God and how to love each other. Throughout this passage, He repeatedly commands the Israelites to remember His faithfulness. This call to remember is our invitation to celebrate who God is, what He has done, and what we trust He will continue to do. These recollections are the footholds that help us understand our place in God's story—a much bigger story than the one that centers on our own striving.

Of all the ancient festivities discussed in the Old Testament, I am particularly intrigued by the Year of Jubilee, which God's people celebrated every fifty years. The festival included cancelling all debts, releasing all slaves, and returning all land and property to its original owners. All of these actions were a jubilant response to the gracious provision of God (Leviticus 25). The acts of returning and releasing were intended to remind God's people of the security they celebrate in God. This tradition was designed to instill a mindset that everything we have belongs to God and that we are merely stewards of the gifts He has given to us, helping them to keep a light touch on material possessions. In releasing their belongings, they had open hands to receive Him in places they may have been tempted to replace Him. They released their possessions to remember His provision. You have to let go before you can receive the next thing.

I am challenged by this idea as someone who likes to collect things that will provide security, including possessions, information, time, and status. For me, the most difficult things to relinquish are my pride, my dreams, and my performance. You might call your treasures by different names: the need for control, the desire for accumulation or upward mobility, social status, or personal recognition. I find it curious, really, that celebration involves so much release. Festivity feels like it should look like *more*—more fanfare, extra decorations, indulgent food, loud music, brighter colors. But instead, we let go of our securities in order to remember the source of our merriment. Celebration doesn't guide us toward greed but gently moves us toward generosity. Through release, we become aware of God's abundance. Once again, we understand that celebration of the self is a life that bends inward. But a celebration of God is a life that leans outward toward the light.

Celebration doesn't guide us toward greed but gently moves us toward generosity.

Maybe that's why I return to the city each week—to remember that the source of my celebration is a person, someone who knows me and loves me and has provided His best for me, including a place that once represented so much loss and disappointment. Our time in the city was a Sabbath of sorts—a rhythm that created space to remember God's astonishing faithfulness and to recall our place in His story. This is what I see today: A skyline that feels more like a welcome banner than a sign that tells me I do not belong. I see two little boys—one wiggling on the monkey bars and another babbling in a swing—who I can hardly believe are real, let alone mine, who I have the privilege of raising and celebrating every day. I see a man walking toward us down 67th Street whom I've spent almost more of my life with than without. I'm grateful for our years together and for the life we are creating under the banner of God's grace. We've walked a lot of different kinds of ground, side by side, sometimes stumbling, but always together.

This is what I know for sure: God's faithfulness never stops being true. But participating in regular celebrations and the rhythm of rituals and traditions are habits to help us remember and rely on God's power and provision. And these festivities, no matter how small, come with a million invitations to let go of what feels safe to receive what will set us free—like monkey bars.

CHAPTER 20

The Source of Celebration

Jesus sat in the midst of joy sipping the coming sorrow, so
we can sit in the midst of sorrow and sip the coming joy.

Timothy Keller

IT WAS SUNDAY AFTERNOON AND our new family of five—including our brand-new daughter, Annie —were doing our best to leave the house and make the fifty-yard trip from our front door to our neighborhood community beach. It seems to me that the preparation and clean up for such trips these days takes longer than the time we actually enjoy Connecticut's shoreline. But I reminded myself that memory-making is a worthy investment and it takes the time it takes. Sometimes the process is the point, I told myself yet again as I rubbed every square inch of my kids' limbs with sunscreen. James, sensing my pending exasperation, said, "Just embrace the wow of now, Mom." I am unsure whether to credit his old soul or *Daniel Tiger's Neighborhood*—a remake of sorts of *Mister Rogers' Neighborhood* and his favorite show. Wherever it came from, I decide it is a good idea and I heed his wisdom. We pack towels for every person in the family, beach toys, spare chairs in case all the Adirondack chairs at the beach are occupied, drinks and snacks, bug spray, and all the supplies needed for a lemonade stand.

James, now five years old, had begged Jimmy and me all summer to have a lemonade stand. In the midst of a full season, it seemed this bucket-list item kept getting pushed out, and today was the day. We decided that taking our lemonade stand to the beach where most of the neighborhood spent the weekend together would be a nice way to engage with the neighbors. Also, we felt that having a few customers would make for a more encouraging experience for James.

When our stroller brigade had made it to the beach, we promptly set up camp, including the much-anticipated lemonade stand: ice, several jugs of lemonade, and a choice of red or blue plastic cups stacked on a picnic table. We had planned to serve complimentary lemonade, but the neighbors insisted on encouraging James's entrepreneurial spirit and began handing him money in exchange for a cup, which of course we refused. Finally, we compromised and allowed the neighbors to pay James in pieces of sea glass—a currency that was more than acceptable to James and one that he was probably more excited about anyway. This started a neighborhood sea-glass hunt on the beach. Adults and kids alike would cheer when they found pieces of sea glass in the sand. Many shared their spoils with fellow neighbors who had yet to spot a piece and promptly brought them to James in exchange for their cold treat. After about forty-five minutes, our neighborhood beach looked like a family-friendly party. I smiled watching James handle each piece of sea glass with reverence and take pride in handing every neighbor, old and young, a cup of lemonade. Together, we celebrated the long days of summer, new friends, and the gift of community. We laughed and made space for play and delighted in the beauty of the boats parading in and out of Long Island Sound.

When the last cup had been poured, James fell into the Adirondack chair next to mine, exhausted, as if he'd reached the chair from the farthest corner of the world. I snuggled sweet Annie, sweaty on my chest as I brushed James's hair away from his tired eyes, keeping one eye fixed on Charlie who was playing with, but mostly consuming, the sand. I watched the bow of a speedboat rip the water into wings of spray. I noticed the sunbeams climb down the oak trees that hovered in the corners of the beach as Long Island Sound pulled its shining sheets over the shore.

It wasn't long ago that this scene—or joy and celebration of any kind, really—would leave me feeling uneasy and afraid, unsure of God's presence in my joy and confused about how to interact with Him in celebration. I'm learning to talk to God with excitement about my dreams, believing that He is eager to hear them and keeping my gaze focused into the future with an expectant heart. I recognize God's presence in both the seemingly mundane and monumental joys in my life. I love celebrating with God instead of seeing celebration as merely the result of the struggles God has carried me through. I talk to God about what brings me delight instead of waiting for desperation to connect us.

IN MY MOST INNOCENT, CHILDLIKE imagination, I see God basking in this scene, elbows nearly touching mine in the Adirondack chair beside me, lifting His face to the warmth of the sun and marveling at the goodness before us. He's laughing with gladness alongside me as He watches me delight in His gifts. He's not surprised by His own abundance and generosity. But He celebrates with me wholeheartedly, and His voice is tender in this joyful place too. He's cheering on my kids—His kids—as they interact with the world He made. Maybe, sitting next to me, He'd watch the boats float in and out of the sound and tell me which one was His personal favorite.

I see now that celebration is not a pathway that leads me away from God. Rather, celebration is essential to God's character and central to His mission. *Where is God in the room?* He is at the center of the celebration.

Jesus made his position as the center and source of our celebration clear during His first miracle when He attended a wedding with His disciples along with His mother, Mary (John 2:1–12).

Before the festivities were over, the hosts ran out of wine, which would have been a tremendous social embarrassment in that culture at the time. Mary was sensitive to the situation and turned to Jesus to make Him aware of the problem to which Jesus replied, "Woman, why do you involve me? . . . My hour has not yet come" (v. 4 NIV).

> *Celebration is essential to God's character and central to His mission.*

At first glance, Jesus' words feel adolescent— reluctant and rebellious somehow as if He's annoyed that His mother has brought this to His attention or had any kind of expectation of Him.

But Jesus' mind wasn't on the present wedding celebration. His gaze was fixed on His own wedding with you and me as His bride. Just as we take communion and see the bread as Christ's body and see the wine as the blood of Christ, Jesus saw the wine as the blood He would soon shed for our sake. In telling His mom that it's not yet His hour, Jesus was thinking of the hour of His death. He was envisioning the blood He would spill in order to unite with us as His bride—a costly celebration.[1]

There were six stone water jars nearby, and shifting to the present moment, Jesus told the servants to fill them to the brim with water. But when the water was drawn from the jars and taken to the master of the wedding feast, it had been turned to wine, making it the first miracle, revealing God's glory.

This story was not merely a miracle of convenience but a purposeful window into God's relationship to celebration.

Whether overtly or covertly, many of us have been given a message that Jesus is above or might even condemn celebration and fun. Many of us have considered Jesus separate from our joy and have somehow been fooled into thinking that the decision to follow Him is to choose to live a life void of festivity. But Jesus does not seek to strip us of celebration. He is the source of celebration! He is the avenue of the greatest joy available to us. Often, we read about God's laws and instruction in the Bible and see a choice between the way of God and a vibrant, joy-filled life. But even God's instruction is not meant to stifle our joy but to usher us into the fullest life possible. In fact, we deprive ourselves of joy when we are hesitant to trust that celebration is essential to Christ's character and that He longs for us to delight in Him and with Him.

As Christians, we often say that Jesus came to suffer for the sake of our sin or to save us from our sin. While true, this is incomplete and far from the central narrative of the gospel. Jesus did indeed endure a painful death for the sake of our sin. But Jesus didn't come to suffer. He was willing to suffer so that we could ultimately celebrate with Him. His suffering was not the aim, but a means to an end. Jesus' first miracle was a wedding. But it was also a sign of the celebration to come: Christ receiving us as His bride with all of our stains and scars (Revelation 19). As the bride, we will be clothed in fine linen—pure and clean—through the blood of Jesus. And we will celebrate that because of Jesus, we are Christ's cherished, glowing bride.

What marks the heart of a person who has put her whole trust in Jesus? How could celebration not be at the top of the list? If we truly understand God's embrace of us as His bride, exuberant joy is the only logical response. To be a Christ-follower is to encounter joy and be a person marked by celebration. To be united with Christ in such an intimate way means that we don't settle for simply knowing about God, but we thoroughly enjoy our relationship with Him and rejoice in what we have in our union with Christ readily. We are invited to cherish His companionship, to rest our heads against His comfort, to delight in His creativity, to dance at the freedom He offers, and to feel secure in His sovereignty. We celebrate that we are safe in God's economy and nothing happens outside of His awareness. We are settled in our identity as God's child and enjoy a radical acceptance where His love outweighs our need for approval from others. We celebrate that by grace, we are His.

To fully celebrate our rich inheritance in Christ, we must recognize that we have nothing apart from Him. Mary didn't tell Jesus that they were running low on wine. She didn't suggest that perhaps it would be prudent to purchase some extra wine to have just in case. It is only when we empty ourselves of false securities that we can be filled with the joy that union with Christ provides.

Jesus is the friend and Father, who is close to both the brokenhearted and to the one who rejoices. This is what gives me the courage to celebrate: knowing that God is present and active in both our sorrow and our celebration.

I LOOKED DOWN AT ANNIE, resting on my chest and snoring louder than I knew a newborn baby could. I call them "snuggle snorts." All of my kids have been particularly loud sleepers as infants, which I consider a grace—a constant assurance that they are here, snuggled in my praising arms. Otherwise, I might not believe it.

My gaze shifted to the sand and my throat tightened. Nearly choking on my own words I said to Jimmy, "Remember that day on the beach last summer when I told you that I was pregnant with Annie?"

Jimmy nodded, remembering that day well.

"I almost wrote a question mark," I whispered.

Just a year prior, we took a family walk on the beach on a Saturday morning. Just before I left the house, I was stunned to discover that I was indeed pregnant. We knew that we wanted to have more children if possible, but our history of miscarriages made this news a very big surprise. I kept the joy to myself as we made our way to the beach. I felt excited. But having endured several losses before the blessing of both James and Charlie, it was difficult to trust the peace and possibility over the pattern. Still, I celebrated, and I hoped.

Unable to contain the news, I let Jimmy and James wander down the beach. As they gingerly lifted rocks and awkwardly stepped around tide pools, looking for hermit crabs and sea glass, I quickly scrawled our boys' initials in the sand with my pointer finger and a *#3* underneath them for Jimmy to see when they meandered back in my direction:

JW

CF

#3

After I finished writing, I paused, debating if I should put a *?* after the *#3*. Part of me felt foolish in celebrating this good but early news. I was tempted to practice disappointment and rehearse our grief instead of celebrating the gift I held in that moment. But I just couldn't put a *?* next to any of my children, whether I would meet them on this side of heaven or the other. As my friend Steph had reminded me with a previous pregnancy, I didn't have permission to grieve this one yet.

Jimmy smiled, his gaze landing on Annie, sleeping contented on my chest. "Well, it looks like God gave us an exclamation point."

I'M LEARNING TO WRITE MORE exclamation points in my life. I'm finding the courage to celebrate. There are times when it feels natural—an automatic response. Other times, it feels uncomfortable. But in my experience, to practice celebration, you don't need it to come naturally. You start where you are and know that your first attempt and probably your first several attempts will be quite poor and feel clunky and awkward.

Celebrate anyway. Celebrate that you had the courage to try a new thing. You gave the goal everything you had. You pushed through the doubt to pursue the dream. Celebrate the people God has put in your path and appreciate the unique ways that they enrich your life. And don't wait until their birthday to let them know. Toast to good news—a promotion, an anniversary, a graduation, a new apartment, being proclaimed "cancer-free," being matched with a child in the long and arduous but beautiful adoption process. Celebrate the gift of waking up to a new day, chock-full of fresh starts and second and third helpings of grace—new mercies.

These celebrations might look like a party with elegant attire, your favorite champagne, and a toast to a major milestone or accomplishment. Or, it may look like pajamas, breakfast for dinner, and roasting marshmallows in the front yard and giving your neighbors an open invitation every Saturday night. Maybe you send a note of affirmation in the mail to a friend without waiting for an occasion to be your excuse to do so. Or perhaps you sit on the floor and pull out the collected notes of encouragement and affirmation you have received over the years to remind yourself of the impact you have had in others' lives. Maybe celebrating looks like receiving the compliments you've been taught you should reject. Perhaps embracing joy simply looks like allowing yourself to feel proud or saying words out loud that are true but sometimes difficult to believe like, "I am a good creation, designed by a good Father." Maybe it means pausing, taking a mental picture of babies crawling all over the floor, the apple sticker that's been stuck to your pants for three hours, and the crayons poured out all over the counter and whispering "thank you" to God as a way of savoring the moments we might be tempted to wish away.

Sometimes celebration comes in a package that looks different than we expected. Often celebration will look like *less*, a *no*, or the end of something good that is no longer right. Maybe it's saying *no* to an opportunity that seems impressive but is incongruent with your needs and values in this season. Or, it might mean choosing to treat yourself with more patience instead of pressuring yourself to push or perform.

It may even look like letting go of what you think you want for what will set you free. These celebrations might go unseen and won't earn you awards. But these are significant celebrations too.

Perhaps you picture a certain profile when you imagine someone who celebrates often and easily and think, *I'm just not a celebrator.* You might feel like celebrating asks you to become someone different—more extraverted, more exuberant, more optimistic, or gifted in event planning. Being a celebrator might ask you to grow, but it also requires that you remain exactly who you are.

Here, I am reminded of a truth one of my professors told our class in graduate school. We had reached the point in our marriage and family therapy master's program in which we were beginning to see clients for the first time—actual people seeking help and often paying a fee for our services! As a class, we were nervous and full of questions for our professor. What questions should we ask first? What should we do if . . . ? What are we supposed to wear? Basically, we wanted a script to follow and a costume to wear that would make us feel secure in the unknown. We wanted our counseling ministries to matter and make a difference.

I'll never forget what my professor said: "When you abandon yourself in favor of who you think you should be as a therapist, you lose your pulse on the Spirit's nudge." God's presence will never leave you. But if you are so preoccupied trying to look the part or be who you think you should be, your ear will be tuned to the voice of approval instead of the prompting of the Holy Spirit.

The same is true for celebration. There's nothing wrong with admiring the talents of others or learning from those who express joy well or differently than we do. But Galatians 1:10 offers a question we can all ask ourselves as we step out to love, lead, and celebrate with others: "Am I now trying to win the approval of human beings, or of God? Or am I trying to please people? If I were still trying to please people, I would not be a servant of Christ" (NIV).

Being a servant of Christ asks you to be the person God made you to be. Celebration won't ask you to change. But it will ask you to be brave with your whole self—to honor others and the life you've been given with gumption.

> *Celebration won't ask you to change. But it will ask you to be brave with the self you were given.*

The world needs our stories of celebration. Revelation 12:11 says, "They triumphed over him by the blood of the Lamb and by the word of their testimony; they did not love their lives so much as to shrink from death" (NIV). Your testimony will include God's movement in your waiting, His redemption in the parts of your life you had written off as ruined, and the grace that you found when you lost the thing you thought you wanted. But there is also powerful testimony in your victory. As Christians on mission in our world, in our culture, in our communities and in our homes, we are fighting from victory—Christ's victory. Let us not be timid in sharing the testimony of Christ's triumph and delight in our wins with joy together. Let's allow our celebration to speak to the God who has given and will always give us a reason to do so.

PERHAPS YOU TOO HAVE ALLOWED fear to govern too many of your years. That fear has made you comfortable in the dark and hypervigilant in the light. Right now, you might be tempted to ask yourself questions like, What if I'm foolish to hope? What if I embrace celebration only to have the joy ripped from my hands?

But this is the truth I want to press into your palms: you—just as you are in this moment—are celebrated. And you are a celebrator. You've been given an invitation to release your fears, choose joy, and find the courage to celebrate. And now, looking bravely toward the future, the question I have for you is, what if it's wonderful?

Don't Wait to Celebrate!

Dear friend,

As a therapist, I love questions. Mostly, I love their ability to forge personal growth and relational connection. I have included several questions here for each chapter, which you can use in many different ways, including for personal reflection in the places and spaces that prompt you to celebrate your everyday life—a sudsy bath, the end of a dock, or in your favorite chair that has memorized your form.

But since this is a book of celebration, may I encourage you to reach out to a group of friends, old or new, and invite them to read and discuss this book together? As I wrote this book and prayed for every person who would read it, I always pictured that the pages would be a bit tattered and stained as it sits in the midst of your celebration. I envisioned chocolate-smudged fingerprints in the margins, rich coffee or peppery wine splattered across the pages, and the subtle run of ink from tears of joy.

Whatever the details of your celebration, my prayer is that each of these questions will be the birthplace of meaningful reflection, honest conversation, and sincere friendship with God and those who have accompanied you on this quest. And I pray that as you remember

God's faithfulness in both the difficult and delightful moments of your life, you will find the courage to celebrate.

Blessings to you, friend!

Nicole

Discussion Guide

Chapter 1: What If It's Wonderful?

1. What has the pain you have experienced in life cost you?
2. What behaviors do you find yourself doing in an attempt to anesthetize painful feelings or protect yourself from hurt?
3. What are some characteristics that you know to be true about God but struggle to trust based on painful circumstances or events in your life?
4. Like the five daughters of Zelophehad, how might God be inviting you to trust His promises over your personal experience?

Chapter 2: Broken Toys

1. How has your pain—your own "broken toys"—been an avenue of growth and grace in your life?
2. How have your painful experiences complicated your relationship with joy and celebration?
3. Where do you picture God in the midst of your pain? Where do you picture Him in the light of your joy?
4. What pain might you be hanging on to simply because it's familiar and comfortable?

Chapter 3: The Shadow of Shame

1. How have your ideas about celebration been shaped by what you earn or deserve?
2. As you consider the apostle Paul's instruction to "take every thought captive" (2 Corinthians 10:5 NRSV), what are some practical ways you can fight for truth in your mind?
3. In what ways are you quick to believe criticism and slow to trust a compliment?
4. What "fig leaves" do you use in your life in order to hide?
5. Reflecting on your life, how has shame shaped your relationship with God and other people?

Chapter 4: Protective Pessimism

1. How have you experienced joy as foreboding or dangerous?
2. What are the ways you have protected yourself from possibility with pessimism?
3. In what ways have you assumed pessimism is a part of your personality rather than emotional reactivity?
4. What difference would it make for you and your relationship with God and others to choose to laugh with delight like Abraham instead of laughing with cynicism like Sarah?
5. Considering your own life, how might God be inviting you to walk the outer boundary of your gifts like Abraham?

Chapter 5: Comparison's Cost

1. When has God asked you to celebrate a dream in someone else's life that you would like to have for yourself? How did the opportunity to celebrate that person feel to you?
2. What has comparison cost you in your own life?

3. How have you experienced the difference between accepting others' gifts and success and celebrating others' gifts and success?
4. In what ways are you prone to give in to the scarcity mentality, assuming that someone's gain is your loss?
5. What difference does it make in your relationship with others when you consider that you have been the recipient of a joy that is anything but fair?

Chapter 6: This Is It?

1. How do you typically respond to opportunities to celebrate gifts and experiences in your life? How are you tempted to minimize your celebration or expect too much joy from your celebration?
2. Consider a time when you expected more joy from an earthly gift or celebration than it was meant to give. How did this displaced celebration impact you spiritually, emotionally, or relationally?
3. What are the potential consequences of your earthly joys "standing awkwardly in the wrong position" in your life?
4. What treasures in your life are currently in the wrong place in your heart or need to be moved off center?

Chapter 7: Where Is Jesus?

1. How have you experienced joy to be an avenue of growth in your life?
2. Considering the story in Luke 1, in what ways are you like Zechariah and in what ways are you like Elizabeth in response to your joy?
3. What does Jesus look like to you in the midst of your joy and celebration?

4. Where is Jesus in the room of your joy?

Chapter 8: Love Lavishly

1. How have you been tempted to consider beauty or fun as frivolous or unimportant?

2. Considering the sinful woman's lavish demonstration of love in the Gospel of Luke, in what ways have you responded like the Pharisees in response to extravagant celebration? In what ways have you responded like Jesus?

3. How have your ideas about spiritual maturity included or excluded the deep delight of God?

4. How has beauty or lavish demonstrations of love in your life led you to encounter Christ?

Chapter 9: Receive Affirmation

1. What messages have you chosen to believe about your identity that have served as a barrier to celebration?

2. In what ways has it required courage for you to stare into the expanse of your belovedness?

3. How have you witnessed both pride and shame causing you to focus on yourself?

4. What would it look like to acknowledge both your failures and your triumphs and celebrate who you are apart from both?

5. How do the stories of creation and the cross set you free to see and celebrate your belovedness?

Chapter 10: Joy in Sadness

1. How have you experienced the interplay between pain and joy in your own life?

2. Like the character Joy from the movie *Inside Out*, what feelings might you be tempted to contain and ignore? How might acknowledging these feelings actually be helpful to you?

3. What difference does it make to your current circumstances to know that Jesus promises that we will rejoice and our joy will not be taken from us?

4. How has sadness helped you find joy in your life?

Chapter 11: The Dance of Grace

1. What messages have you received throughout your life about celebrating triumphs or victories?

2. How does knowing God as the source of your blessing encourage you to choose joy and find the courage to celebrate?

3. How does David's exuberant worship change your ideas about celebration?

4. In what ways are you tempted to respond to others' celebration like Michal in 2 Samuel 6?

5. How might your hesitancy to celebrate be a sign that you have made your gifts and accomplishments about you?

Chapter 12: Hope in the Middle

1. How have you struggled to choose joy in the "middle place"—between where you've been and where you would like to be?

2. What are some of the "shoulds" you often speak to yourself?

3. How has learning someone's story helped you understand his or her pain differently?

4. How does knowing Christ's ultimate victory as the end of

the story allow you to see your pain in the middle place differently?

Chapter 13: Joining Others' Joy

1. What invitations do you have to love your family members or people in your community by celebrating what they love?
2. What does the apostle Paul's instruction to allow our lives to be interrupted by others' mourning or rejoicing look like in your life?
3. How has the practice of loving others by celebrating their loves allowed you to experience joy you might not encounter on your own?

Chapter 14: Keep the Thank-You Notes

1. How have you experienced the gift of expressing thankfulness beyond simply feeling grateful? How did it shape you personally?
2. Where do you see yourself in the story of the ten lepers from Luke 17?
3. How does it shape your ideas about gratitude to consider thankfulness as means of celebration with God?
4. What are some ways that thankfulness has improved your sense of well-being?
5. What are some ways you can "keep the thank-you notes" in your own life?

Chapter 15: Practice Savoring

1. How might the practice of savoring help you deepen your celebration of the ordinary gifts God has provided in your life?

2. Considering the Psalm's invitation to "Taste and see that the LORD is good" (Psalm 34:8 NIV), how can you use your five senses to savor and celebrate the life God has given you?

3. What are some ways you can accept Jesus' invitation to choose "the better thing" and savor time with Him?

4. How have you experienced laughter as a form of celebration in your life?

5. What would it look like to cement your celebration by sharing it with others?

Chapter 16: Be Expectant

1. When have you found your delight in Christ to be dependent upon your circumstances?

2. In what ways have you merely sipped on God's faithfulness by limiting your awe of God?

3. What are some opportunities in your life right now to have an expectant heart by knowing that God can, believing that He will, and trusting His goodness regardless of the outcome?

4. How can you cultivate joy in the future by celebrating the life you are living now?

Chapter 17: Share the Good News

1. What difference does it make in your joy when you share your good news with others?

2. How has sharing with others about the difference Christ has made in your life increased your joy?

3. In what ways have you experienced joy in your weakness when you depend on Christ? How do your vulnerability and limitations prompt you to celebrate?

Chapter 18: Learn to Play

1. How has hunting for beauty and delight kept you tethered to God's story?
2. What difference does it make to understand celebration as a discipline rather than simply a reflex?
3. In what ways have you passively been waiting for God to inject you with joy? What would it look like for you to become an active participant?
4. How have you experienced the difference between celebration and escape?
5. What differences between joy and pleasure-seeking have you witnessed and experienced?
6. Name five delights that are present in your life right now.

Chapter 19: Rhythms and Rituals

1. What rituals help you celebrate your relationship with God and other people?
2. What are some potential barriers to your practicing these rituals regularly?
3. How do rituals help you release your control and celebrate God's provision?
4. How might celebration be an invitation for you to release false securities in your life?
5. What is the difference between rhythms and rituals being our "help" versus our "hope"?

Chapter 20: The Source of Celebration

1. Reflecting on your own life, what are the messages you've received about God's view of celebration?

2. After reading this book, where do you picture God in the midst of your joy and celebration?
3. How does Jesus' character and His mission here on earth increase your courage to celebrate?
4. How is God inviting you to ask yourself, what if it's wonderful?

Acknowledgments

SOME BOOKS ARE WRITTEN ON the other side of personal transformation. They're before-and-after stories. This book is not one of them. I wrote my way through these trials and triumphs, and as I wrestled with the truths in these pages, I had a team of people—a family, really, asking me the question, what if it's wonderful?

Jess Connolly, when I asked you to pray that I would find the courage to celebrate and your eyes grew wide and you said, "I think that's your next book," your words were God's invitation to me to a new way of living. Thank you for pouring courage into my heart as I learned to live and share this message.

To my brilliant literary agent and dear friend, Angela—you are God's kindness to me. Your presence and partnership during every stage of this project were an invaluable gift to me and the work itself. Thank you for encouraging me to lean on the truth that I knew, but often struggled to trust. I love you and am grateful for you.

To the kind and capable W Publishing team—what a privilege to work with you! It's a gift to be one of yours.

Special thanks to Debbie Wickwire. It is an embarrassment of riches to have the opportunity to work with you as my editor. I love you, Friend. Thank you for your "yes" and for championing me both personally and professionally. Stay in touch! XO!

Much gratitude for Dawn Hollomon. I feel like we are kindred spirits and we've become fast friends. It's a delight to work with you. I'm excited for all that is to come!

Tom Dean, I will never forget the email you sent me. Your encouragement and extravagant generosity were winks from God when I needed them most and a reflection of God's lavish love. Thank you, Friend. It is a JOY to work with you.

Joel Muddamale, I love learning from you! Your passion for God's Word is inspiring and contagious and your abundant wisdom was invaluable to these pages. It's an honor to work with you and call you, "Friend."

Shanon, I love seeing your name on my calendar. Every phone call with you feels like a hug. Thank you for your excitement about this message and for helping me share the good news with others.

To Caleb Peavy and the Unmutable team—I feel so much joy in seeing God's creativity reflected in people whose gifts are so different than my own. I am in awe!

Terry and Sharon Hargrave, one of my life's greatest gifts is calling you mentors and friends. I love you both and it's a joy to be "covered in your dust." Keep the thank-you notes!

Margot Starbuck, you're so much fun. I'm eternally grateful for your honest feedback that somehow always comes wrapped in the most enthusiastic encouragement.

Greg, your discipleship has been transformational for me. Thank you from the bottom of my heart.

Lindsay, thank you for being safe enough to be a "dangerous" friend. Our friendship is rare and, frankly, one of the most beautiful gifts I've ever received. The truths tucked inside this book are in large part the fruit of conversations I've had with you. Thank you for your loving wisdom.

Barb, thank you for being an "Aaron" friend—you've lifted my arms with your prayers, scripture, discerning words, laughter, hugs, and conversation throughout the living and writing of this message. I love you and am grateful for you.

Blair, thank you for your careful reading of this manuscript, and for pressing hope into my hands with the question, what if it's wonderful? You are a safe harbor. The first chapter says it all.

Berit, you're so special to us and living proof that God writes the very best stories. Thank you for your tender care and for loving on each of us so well as I worked on this project.

Danielle, thank you for sharing your own version of this story with me. I treasure our deep and honest friendship.

Shauna, you've already shaped my story in significant ways. Our friendship is new, but runs deep. I'm grateful for you.

Megan Marshman, thank you for your willingness to help me wrestle with God's Word and process my feelings in response. Even from a distance, you have made this book richer.

Megan Kelly, no matter where I find myself standing on a given day as a person and as a writer, you seem to understand and have the ability to make me feel less alone across state lines.

Tayler, thank you for your steadfast encouragement and tender truth-telling. I needed a cheerleader on the sidelines for this one and you graciously agreed to play that vital role.

To the many friends who have helped me find the courage to celebrate and to not be afraid of joy's plenty—Elisabeth S. Shirley, Halley Anne, Steph, Tori, Jeannie, Elisabeth H., Kelley, Vicky, Paige, Christine, Libby, Susan, Desi, Phoebe, Krista, Ben, Anne, Theta, Tim C., and Tim S.

To our Trinity Church family, your fingerprints are smudged all over these stories. Special thanks to Ben Valentine for generously sharing your excitement about this message and the insights that helped shape it.

Heartfelt thanks to my clients—you will never know how much I learn from you. Thank you for sharing your stories with me. It's an honor to be a part of your journey.

Much gratitude for the Zasowski Family. Thank you for constant affirmation and celebration of me . . . you are fiercely loyal and love me so well.

Love and special thanks to my parents, Chuck and Gigi Wallace, for showing me the JOY of having a relationship with Jesus. You provided the blueprints of celebration I'm returning to in this season. I love you, and it's a tremendous gift to be your daughter.

Buckets of gratitude for my sisters, Brianna and Laura Anne, my built-in best friends. I treasure you as prized and precious gifts in my life.

Jimmy, you celebrate my gifts like they are your own. Thank you for seeing the significance of this message and bearing witness to its work in my life. Thank you for making space in our time, energy, and finances to support my call to share it. It's the gift of my life to celebrate God's goodness together with you. I love you.

James, Charlie, and Annie, it's a delight to be your Mama. James, I celebrate your tender heart, creative curiosity, and thoughtfulness. Charlie, I celebrate your affectionate nature, determination, and joy. Annie, I celebrate your sweet spirit, peaceful presence, and your easy smile.

Finally, I'm thankful for You, Jesus. You are so good to me. My earnest prayer is that these pages bring You honor and glory. This book is my joyful noise to You.

Notes

Chapter 3: The Shadow of Shame

1. Rick Hanson, *Buddha's Brain: The Practical Neuroscience of Happiness, Love, and Wisdom* (Berkely: New Harbinger, 2009).

2. Roy F. Baumeister, Ellen Bratslavsky, Catrin Finkenauer, and Kathleen D. Vohs, "Bad is stronger than good," *Review of General Psychology* 5, no. 4 (December 2001), 323–370.

3. David J. Williams, *Paul's Metaphors: Their Context and Character* (Peabody, MA: Hendrickson Publishers, 1999), 216.

4. Victor Paul Furnish, II *Corinthians: Translated with Introduction, Notes, and Commentary*, vol. 32a, *The Anchor Bible* (New Haven: Yale University Press, 2008), 458.

5. Terry D. Hargave, Nicole E. Zasowski, and Miyoung Yoon Hammer, *Advances and Techniques in Restoration Therapy* (New York: Routledge, 2019), 163.

6. Terry D. Hargrave, Nicole E. Zasowski, and Miyoung Yoon Hammer, *Advances and Techniques in Restoration Therapy* (New York: Routledge, 2019), 17.

Chapter 4: Protective Pessimism

1. Francine Shapiro, *Eye Movement Desensitization and Reprocessing (EMDR) Therapy*, 3rd Edition (New York: The Guilford Press, 2018), 39.

2. OWN, "Dr. Brené Brown on Joy: It's Terrifying," YouTube video, March 17, 2013, https://www.youtube.com/watch ?v=RKV0BWSPfOw&t=4s.

Chapter 5: Comparison's Cost
1. C.S. Lewis, *Mere Christianity*, (San Francisco: HarperOne, 2001).

Chapter 8: Love Lavishly
1. Rick Renner, *Sparkling Gems from the Greek* (Tulsa, OK: Harrison House Publishers, 2003), 610.
2. Grant R. Osborne, *Matthew*, vol. 1, *Zondervan Exegetical Commentary on the New Testament* (Grand Rapids, MI: Zondervan, 2010), 950.
3. W. Günther and G.-H. Link, "Love," ed. Lothar Coenen, Erich Beyreuther, and Hans Bietenhard, *New International Dictionary of New Testament Theology* (Grand Rapids, MI: Zondervan, 1986), 539.

Chapter 9: Receive Affirmation
1. Terry Hargrave and Sharon Hargrave, *5 Days to New Self* (self-pub, 2016), Cenveo-Trafton Printing, 51.
2. Timothy Keller, *The Freedom of Self-Forgetfulness* (10Publishing, 2012), 32.

Chapter 10: Joy in Sadness
1. Pete Docter, dir., *Inside Out*. 2015; Burbank, CA: Walt Disney Pictures, www.disneyplus.com/movies/inside- out/uzQ2ycVDi2IE.
2. Docter, 21:36.
3. Docter, 1:21:34.
4. Rodney A. Whitacre, John, vol. 4, *The IVP New Testament Commentary Series*, ed. Grant R. Osborne. (Downers Grove, IL: InterVarsity Press, 1999), 394.
5. Sonja Lyubomirsky, *The How of Happiness: A New Approach to Getting the Life You Want* (New York: Penguin Books, 2007).
6. Martin E. P. Seligman, Tracy A. Steen, Nansook Park, and Christopher Peterson, "Positive psychology progress: empirical

validation of interventions," *American Psychologist* 60, no. 5 (July– August 2005).

Chapter 14: Keep the Thank-You Notes

1. Lois Tverberg, "Covered in the Dust of Your Rabbi: An Urban Legend?" January 27, 2012, blog, https://ourrabbijesus.com /covered-in-the-dust-of-your-rabbi-an-urban-legend/.
2. David E. Garland, *Luke*, vol. 3, *Zondervan Exegetical Commentary Series: New Testament*, ed. Clinton E. Arnold. (Grand Rapids, MI: Zondervan, 2011), 689.
3. David P. Wright and Richard N. Jones, "Leprosy," ed. David Noel Freedman, *The Anchor Yale Bible Dictionary* (New York: Doubleday, 1992), 279–280.
4. James R. Edwards, *The Gospel according to Luke,* ed. D. A. Carson, *The Pillar New Testament Commentary* (Grand Rapids, MI; Cambridge, U.K.; Nottingham, U.K.: William B. Eerdmans Publishing Company; Apollos, 2015), 483–484.
5. David E. Garland, *Luke, Zondervan Exegetical Commentary on the New Testament* (Grand Rapids, MI: Zondervan, 2012), 690.
6. Alan Carr, *Positive Psychology and You: A Self-Development Guide* (New York: Routledge, 2020), 143.
7. Carr, 15.
8. Martin E. P. Seligman, Tracy A. Steen, Nansook Park, and Christopher Peterson, "Positive psychology progress: empirical validation of interventions," *American Psychologist* 60, no. 5. (July-August 2005).

Chapter 15: Practice Savoring

1. Carr, *Positive Psychology and You*, 120.
2. Carr, 122–123.
3. Carr, 126
4. Carr, 15.

Chapter 17: Share the Good News

1. I. H. Marshall, A. R. Millard, J. I. Packer, and D. J. Wiseman, *New Bible Dictionary* 3rd Edition (Nottingham, England: Inter-Varsity Press, 1996), 615.
2. Studio 360, "Intentional Flaws," *The World*, July 13, 2002, https://theworld.org/stories/2002-07-13/intentional-flaws.

Chapter 18: Learn to Play

1. Adam Geiger, *Life in Color with David Attenborough*, Netflix, 2021, https://www.netflix.com/watch/81094026?trackId=14170286, 39:52.

Chapter 20: The Source of Celebration

1. Tim Keller Sermon, "Lord of the Wine," November 17, 2006, Series: The Real Jesus Part 2; His Life.

About the Author

NICOLE ZASOWSKI IS A LICENSED marriage and family therapist and the author of *From Lost to Found*. As an old soul who wears her heart proudly on her sleeve, she enjoys writing and speaking on topics that merge her professional knowledge, faith, and personal experience. Nicole lives in Connecticut with her husband and their three young children.